D0246756

MASTERCHEF
GOES LARGE

BECOME AN EXPERT CHEF IN YOUR OWN KITCHEN

TED SMART

CONTENTS

Introduction by John Torode

Masterchef is back but not in the way you might have expected. This time *Masterchef Goes Large*, with 100 contestants being put through their paces, tested and retested to find the ultimate Masterchef 2005.

The challenge was not just for the contestants but also for Gregg and me as judges. How were we going to select people, take them on a culinary journey, inspire and teach them, then judge them? My personal quest was to find someone who not only knew how to cook but, more importantly, had that special spark that would make them stand out head and shoulders above the rest.

The process of judging any competition is never easy unless you set stringent guidelines. For *Masterchef*, we were trying to find someone who could move from the world of the home cook to the world of the professional. So what does it take to be a top chef?

Besides the ability to cook with originality and flair, you need a good understanding of produce and an almost instinctive grasp of the science of cooking: why things work and why they do not. You also need drive and stamina – the ability to hold your own in a tough, hot and pressurised environment. You have to be dedicated not just to food but to your customers. When all is said and done, the professional chef is ruled by the punters and, without their support and approval, failure is a sure thing. Many chefs have come a cropper by being too self-indulgent and not taking into account what their customers want. So lastly, you have to be hospitable, with a talent for making people happy.

Roast Tomato and Red Pepper Soup with Chorizo and Borlotti Beans

The name of this recipe does not do it justice. This is one of those fantastic dishes that you don't except much from initially as it is only a soup, but it gives a massive delivery. The depth of flavour from the chorizo is the main reason for its success. The beans give a great texture and a solid base to what is a wonderful Sunday-evening soup.

→ 400G (14OZ) TOMATOES, CUT INTO QUARTERS
→ 2 RED PEPPERS, CUT INTO LARGE CHUNKS
→ 5 TBSP OLIVE OIL
→ 75G (3OZ) CHORIZO SAUSAGE, CUT INTO SLICES 5MM (¼ IN) THICK
→ 2 LARGE GARLIC CLOVES, FINELY CHOPPED
→ 1 RED CHILLI, FINELY CHOPPED
→ 400G (14OZ) TIN OF BORLOTTI BEANS, DRAINED AND RINSED
→ 500ML (18FL OZ) HOT VEGETABLE STOCK
→ 4 THICK SLICES OF CIABATTA BREAD
→ SALT AND FRESHLY GROUND BLACK PEPPER

1 Preheat the oven to 200°C/400°F/Gas Mark 6.

2 Put the tomatoes and red peppers in a roasting tin. Season with salt and pepper and toss with 3 tablespoons of the olive oil. Roast for 30–40 minutes, until browned around the edges.

3 Meanwhile, heat the remaining olive oil in a frying pan and gently fry the chorizo in it for 3 minutes. Stir in the garlic and chilli and cook for 2 minutes longer. Remove from the heat and stir in the beans, then set aside.

4 Remove the roasted vegetables from the oven and put them into a blender or food processor with half the vegetable stock. Purée until almost smooth.

5 Pour the mixture into a large saucepan. Add the remaining stock and the chorizo and bean mixture and simmer for 5 minutes.

6 Toast the bread. Divide the soup between 4 bowls and serve with the toast.

'What does it take to make a star chef? Ability, charisma, stamina, food knowledge and most of all, passion.'
John Torode, Masterchef Judge

Cauliflower Soup

Cauliflower soup is an old-fashioned favourite that deserves a revival. The classic cauliflower soup is called crème du Barry, and is said to be named after the comtesse du Barry, a favourite mistress of Louis XV of France.

- → 100G (4OZ) BUTTER
- → 1 ONION, FINELY CHOPPED
- → 1 CELERY STICK, CHOPPED
- → 2 POTATOES, PEELED AND FINELY DICED
- → 450G (1LB) CAULIFLOWER, DIVIDED INTO FLORETS
- → 250G (9OZ) PARSNIPS, FINELY DICED
- → 500ML (18FL OZ) CHICKEN OR VEGETABLE STOCK
- → 250ML (8FL OZ) MILK
- → A FEW SPRIGS OF THYME
- → 2 BAY LEAVES
- → 60ML (2FL OZ) DRY VERMOUTH
- → 100ML (3½FL OZ) DOUBLE CREAM
- → 4 QUAIL'S EGGS
- → A GOOD PINCH OF CAYENNE PEPPER
- → 1 TBSP SNIPPED CHIVES
- → SALT AND WHITE PEPPER

1 Melt the butter in a large saucepan, add all the vegetables, then cover and sweat for 6–7 minutes, until soft but not coloured.

2 Add the stock, milk, thyme and bay leaves. Bring to the boil, then reduce the heat, cover and simmer for 20 minutes. Remove the bay leaves.

3 Purée the soup until smooth and season to taste. Add the vermouth and double cream and reheat the soup, but don't let it boil.

4 Poach the quail's eggs (see tip below) until they are cooked but still soft in the centre. Remove with a slotted spoon and drain on kitchen paper.

5 Ladle the soup into 4 warm bowls. Carefully place a poached quail's egg in each bowl. Sprinkle with a little cayenne pepper and the snipped chives and serve immediately.

MASTERCHEF TOP TIP
To poach quail's eggs, place a pan of water over a high heat and bring to a simmer. Pour 100ml (3½fl oz) white wine vinegar into a cup, then break 4 quail's eggs into it. Pour the eggs and vinegar into the water – the eggs will separate from each other. Leave for 2 minutes, then remove from the water with a slotted spoon and drain on kitchen paper. The eggs will be perfectly cooked.
John Torode, Masterchef Judge

'I don't think you're trying to win Masterchef – you're aiming for your first Michelin star!'
Gregg Wallace, Masterchef Judge, to James Cross

Inspired by contestant Fabian Petitcolas

Butternut Squash Soup with Poppy Seed Cream

This simple little soup is completely uplifted by the addition of a poppy seed cream that sits neatly in the centre. The trick is not to have the bowls too hot or the cream will melt. The little croûtons are also known as sippets and are classically served as an accompaniment to dainty soups such as this one.

→ 400G (14OZ) BUTTERNUT SQUASH, PEELED, DESEEDED AND CUT INTO CHUNKS
→ 200ML (7FL OZ) CHICKEN STOCK
→ 40G (1½OZ) BUTTER
→ LEMON JUICE, TO TASTE
→ A DASH OF TABASCO SAUCE
→ 5 TBSP WHIPPING CREAM
→ 2 TSP POPPY SEEDS
→ 1 TBSP OLIVE OIL
→ 3 SLICES OF WHITE BREAD, CUT INTO 5MM–1CM (¼–½ IN) CUBES
→ SALT AND WHITE PEPPER

1 Put the squash into a large saucepan and add the chicken stock, 25g (1oz) of the butter and 200ml (7fl oz) water. Bring to the boil, then reduce the heat and simmer until the squash is tender.

2 Blend until smooth, adding more water if the soup is too thick. Season with lemon juice, Tabasco and some salt and pepper.

3 Whip the cream and poppy seeds together until thick, then set aside.

4 Melt the remaining butter in a large frying pan with the oil. Add the bread cubes and fry over a high heat until crisp and golden all over. Set aside.

5 Reheat the soup to just simmering; do not let it boil. Pour it into 4 soup bowls and carefully place a tablespoon of the poppy seed cream in the centre of each one. Serve immediately, accompanied by the bread croûtons.

Inspired by contestant Vivian Pei

Rich Cream of Fennel Soup with Crab and Red Pepper Coulis

Originally this soup-come-sauce was presented in martini glasses – pretty but not very practical. It would be wise to serve this very rich soup in small quantities, perhaps as a pre-dinner treat. Although there is a lot of work involved, it is well worth it.

→ 15G (½OZ) BUTTER
→ 1 GARLIC CLOVE, CHOPPED
→ 1 FENNEL BULB, FINELY SLICED
→ 1 LEEK (WHITE PART ONLY), FINELY SLICED
→ 1 FLOURY POTATO, SUCH AS
   MARIS PIPER, PEELED AND DICED
→ 1 BAY LEAF
→ ABOUT 175ML (6FL OZ) CHICKEN
   OR VEGETABLE STOCK
→ 1 TSP PERNOD (OPTIONAL)
→ 3 TBSP DOUBLE CREAM
→ 50G (2OZ) FRESH CRAB MEAT
   (A MIXTURE OF WHITE AND BROWN)
→ SALT AND WHITE PEPPER
→ SPRIGS OF DILL, TO GARNISH
   For the red pepper coulis:
→ 15G (½OZ) BUTTER
→ 1 RED PEPPER, CHOPPED
→ 2 TBSP DOUBLE CREAM
→ 1 TBSP TOMATO PURÉE
→ A PINCH OF CAYENNE PEPPER

1 Melt the butter in a saucepan, add the garlic, fennel and leek, then cover and sweat until soft and translucent.

2 Add the potato and bay leaf and pour in enough stock just to cover the vegetables. Cover and simmer for 15–20 minutes, until all the vegetables are tender.

3 Remove the bay leaf and purée the soup until smooth. Pour through a sieve into a clean saucepan and reheat. Stir in the Pernod, if using, and the cream, then season to taste. Cover and keep warm.

4 For the coulis, melt the butter in a small saucepan, add the red pepper and cook over a low heat for 2 minutes. Stir in the cream and tomato purée and season with salt, pepper and the cayenne. Cook over a medium heat for about 10 minutes, stirring occasionally, until the pepper is soft.

5 Purée the mixture in a food processor or liquidiser, then pass it through a sieve into a clean pan. Reheat gently.

6 Spoon a good tablespoon or two of the coulis into 4 glass, ramekin-sized dishes, about 200ml (7fl oz) in capacity. Sprinkle the crab meat over the coulis, then gently spoon the fennel soup over the crab so as not to disturb the layers. Garnish with a sprig of dill. Eat with a teaspoon, scooping through all the layers at once.

Masterchef Masterclass
John Torode's Hollandaise

Hollandaise is one of the great classic sauces. Once you have mastered it you will be able to make any number of variations, including béarnaise (see page 108). A luxurious emulsion of butter and egg yolks flavoured with lemon juice, hollandaise has a reputation for being difficult because of its tendency to separate. However, as long as you don't overheat it, it should be quite safe. The method opposite may seem long and complicated but it's really worth doing. With a little practice, the whole process should take no longer than fifteen minutes, and it helps to build up your muscles!

Traditionally hollandaise is served warm as an accompaniment to vegetables, fish or eggs. It doesn't keep well, so is best made at the last minute. However, you can keep it warm for up to half an hour if necessary by placing the bowl in a large bowl of warm water or by pouring the sauce into a Thermos flask.

Here are the main points to remember when making hollandaise sauce:
→ For the best flavour, use good-quality, fresh unsalted butter.
→ Whisk the egg yolks thoroughly with the vinegar reduction so that the mixture becomes thick and creamy. This helps to stabilise the mixture once you start adding the butter, so the sauce is less likely to separate.
→ Add the butter very slowly at first, then once the mixture has thickened you can speed it up a little.
→ Never overheat hollandaise. The temperature should not exceed 66°C/150°F.
→ If, despite your best efforts, it does look as if it's about to separate, quickly whisk in a tablespoon of hot water. If this doesn't work, you can start again by repeating steps 1 and 2 opposite and gradually whisking in the curdled mixture (you will have a very rich sauce!).

John Torode's
Basic Hollandaise Sauce

SERVES 6
→ 6 TBSP WHITE WINE
→ 6 TBSP WHITE WINE VINEGAR
→ 20 BLACK PEPPERCORNS
→ 2 BAY LEAVES
→ 3 EGG YOLKS
→ 300G (11OZ) WARM MELTED BUTTER
→ A PINCH OF SALT
→ JUICE OF ½ LEMON

1 Put the white wine and vinegar into a small pan with the peppercorns and bay leaves. Bring to the boil and simmer until reduced to about 3 tablespoons. Leave to cool, then remove the peppercorns and bay leaves.

2 Put the egg yolks into a large, heatproof glass bowl and place it over a pan of barely simmering water, making sure the water isn't touching the base of the bowl. Whisk in about a tablespoon of the vinegar reduction and continue to whisk for 2–3 minutes, until the mixture turns pale and thick and the whisk leaves a trail on the surface when lifted (this is known as the ribbon stage).

3 Remove the bowl from the heat and put it on a folded cloth (to stop it slipping and to keep the heat in) on a work surface. Little by little, whisk in the melted butter, making sure each addition is completely incorporated before adding any more. Keep going until all the butter has been used up and the sauce is thick and creamy. Have a bowl of hot water handy so that you can add a tablespoon if you feel that the sauce might be about to scramble.

4 The finished hollandaise should be a light, pourable consistency. Beat in the salt and lemon juice to taste, then serve.

#
John Torode's Asparagus with Hollandaise Sauce

SERVES 6
→ 60 ASPARAGUS SPEARS
→ 1 QUANTITY OF HOLLANDAISE
  SAUCE (SEE PAGE 21)
→ SALT

If you want to talk classic, here we are. Like tomato and basil or strawberries and cream, asparagus and hollandaise were made for each other. Buy the freshest possible asparagus, preferably English, which is in season in May and June, and cook it on the same day.

1 The spears have a tough base and a tender stem and tip. Towards the base, where the green starts to turn to white, they will snap naturally. Break each one individually and discard the bases (or save them to make soup). Use twine to tie the asparagus in bundles of 12 or thereabouts. Don't tie them too tight or you will damage them.

2 Make the hollandaise sauce as described on page 21 and keep warm.

3 Fill a large pot with cold water (or a small amount of water in an asparagus steamer, if you have one) and bring to the boil. Add a good teaspoon of salt, then drop in the asparagus bundles. Return to the boil and start checking whether it's tender after 2 minutes.

4 Remove the asparagus from the pan, cut the twine from each bundle and trim the ends of the spears so they are an even length. Drain very thoroughly, then divide between 6 large, warm serving plates and serve straight away, with the hollandaise sauce.

Inspired by contestant Michael Jones

Pears with Roquefort, Rocket and Pickled Walnuts

This is a delicious combination of flavours, and there are several options for the presentation. For example, you could simply slice the pears and crumble the blue cheese over them, then make a dressing with the lemon and mascarpone. Be sure to include the pickled walnuts. They're a real treat.

→ 4 RIPE WILLIAM PEARS
→ JUICE OF 1 LEMON
→ 100G (4OZ) ROQUEFORT CHEESE
→ 100G (4OZ) MASCARPONE CHEESE
→ 200G (7OZ) WILD ROCKET
→ 3 TBSP EXTRA VIRGIN OLIVE OIL
→ A LITTLE GOOD-QUALITY AGED
  BALSAMIC VINEGAR
→ 16 PICKLED WALNUTS, DRAINED
→ SEA SALT AND FRESHLY GROUND
  BLACK PEPPER

1 Peel the pears, if liked, and remove the cores, leaving a fairly large cavity. Put the pears in a dish and squeeze the lemon juice over them.

2 Mix the Roquefort and mascarpone cheese together and season with plenty of freshly ground black pepper. Pipe the mixture into the pear cavities, or use a small teaspoon to stuff them.

3 Divide the rocket between 4 plates and sit a stuffed pear in the centre of each one.

4 Drizzle the oil and balsamic vinegar over the rocket and scatter the pickled walnuts around. Season with a little sea salt and black pepper and serve immediately.

Masterchef Masterclass
John Torode's Pasta

I know that it's easy to buy pasta and people generally can't be bothered with making it at home, but it is very satisfying to do. Once you know the basics, you can make all sorts of parcels and shapes. Although most of the dried pasta available in shops is of good quality, the vacuum-packed 'fresh' pasta is nothing like the stuff you can make yourself. Proper home-made fresh pasta is rich in eggs and has a lovely, supple texture.

It speeds up the process if you have a hand-cranked pasta machine for rolling out the dough (though with a bit of elbow grease, you can manage with a long rolling pin). A pasta machine is not expensive and it helps you to produce long, thin sheets of pasta in just a few minutes. It fixes to the worktop with a metal clamp and you then pass the dough between rollers until it reaches the thickness you require. There are also special cutters for producing ribbon shapes, such as pappardelle, fettuccine and tagliatelle.

Here are some guidelines for making successful pasta:

→ Use Italian '00' (doppio zero) flour, available in delicatessens and some supermarkets. It is high in gluten, whereas softer flours absorb too much liquid and the pasta may not be strong enough.
→ Pasta dough should be firm but not stiff and crumbly. If it is too soft, mix in a little more flour, a tablespoon at a time; if it is too stiff, mix in a little more egg or olive oil.
→ Cook pasta in a very large pan of boiling salted water, so it has plenty of room to move around and won't stick.
→ Fresh pasta cooks very quickly – sometimes in under a minute – so start checking it as soon as the water has returned to the boil.

John Torode's
Basic Pasta

MAKES ABOUT 600G (1lB 5OZ)

→ 500G (1LB 2OZ) ITALIAN '00' FLOUR,
   PLUS EXTRA FOR DUSTING
→ A PINCH OF TABLE SALT
→ 4 EGGS PLUS 3 EGG YOLKS,
   LIGHTLY BEATEN TOGETHER
→ 1 TBSP OLIVE OIL

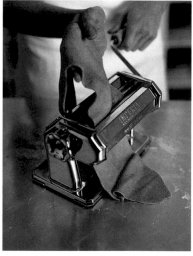

1 Put the flour and salt into a food processor, add half the egg mixture and whiz until incorporated. Add the oil and whiz again.

2 Start to add the rest of the eggs a little at a time, stopping the machine regularly to feel the texture of the mixture. When it is ready, it will be like large, loose breadcrumbs that will come together into a dough if you squeeze them between your fingertips. You may not need to use all the egg, or you may even need to add a little more.

3 Tip the mixture out on to a floured work surface and push together into a ball. Knead for 1–2 minutes by pushing it away with the heel of your hand, folding it over and giving it a quarter turn. It should be smooth and elastic. Wrap in cling film and leave to rest for an hour.

4 Divide the dough into 6 pieces. Re-wrap 5 of them in cling film, then roll out the remaining one in a hand-cranked pasta machine. To do this, put the rollers of the machine on the widest setting. Flatten the piece of dough slightly, then run it through the machine 3 or 4 times, folding it in half each time and giving it a half turn before putting it through the machine again. The dough should become progressively smooth and silky. If it starts to stick, dust it lightly with flour. Repeat with the remaining pieces of dough.

5 Now feed each piece of dough through the machine without folding it, lowering the setting one notch at a time until you reach the required thickness (it's not usually necessary to go to the lowest setting).

6 Cut the rolled pasta into whatever shape you like; you can use the pasta machine attachment to cut them into ribbons.

John Torode's Pappardelle with Chicken Liver Sauce

SERVES 6

→ 600G (1LB 5OZ) FRESH PASTA (SEE OPPOSITE)
→ 3 TBSP OLIVE OIL
→ 500G (1LB 2OZ) CHICKEN LIVERS, TRIMMED
→ 2 ONIONS, SLICED
→ 2 SPRIGS OF OREGANO, CHOPPED
→ 1 RED CHILLI, FINELY CHOPPED
→ 3 GARLIC CLOVES, FINELY CHOPPED
→ 2 X 400G (14OZ) CANS OF TOMATOES, COARSELY CHOPPED
→ 1 GLASS OF RED WINE
→ A GOOD HANDFUL OF PARSLEY, CHOPPED
→ 15G (½OZ) BUTTER
→ SALT AND FRESHLY GROUND BLACK PEPPER
→ FRESHLY GRATED PARMESAN CHEESE, TO SERVE

Pasta and chicken livers may seem a little weird but it is actually a very old combination. You may have come across bruschetta or crostini topped with chopped chicken livers. This sauce is based on the same principle but then mixed with wonderful, thick-cut fresh pasta. You could also serve it with gnocchi.

1 Roll out the pasta as described opposite and cut it into pappardelle (strips about 2cm (³/4 in) wide).

2 Heat 2 tablespoons of the olive oil in a large frying pan, add the chicken livers and fry over a fairly high heat for about 1 minute. Toss well and fry for 2 minutes longer, until well coloured and crisp on the outside but still pink on the inside. Remove from the pan and set aside.

3 Add the remaining olive oil to the pan and add the onions and oregano. Fry until the onions are translucent, then add the chilli and garlic and fry for another minute. Stir in the chopped tomatoes, red wine and some salt and pepper. Simmer for 5 minutes, stirring frequently, then increase the heat to high and cook for a minute or two longer, until the sauce thickens.

4 Cook the pasta in a large pan of boiling salted water until *al dente* (tender but firm to the bite), then drain. Set aside, with the warm pan.

5 Chop the livers roughly and add to the sauce with the parsley. Taste and adjust the seasoning.

6 Return the pasta to the warm pan and toss with the butter, then add the sauce and toss well. Serve with Parmesan cheese.

Name: Anna Mosesson
Age: 48
Occupation: I am a Borough Market stall holder (I have been for 6 years), I sell Scandinavian food.
Place of residence: Suffolk
Why did you apply to Masterchef?
My son was at the market with me, and he saw these bits of paper being handed out and said, 'Mamma! I think you should go for this!', so I did. A lot of people I know said, 'This is it, it's your open door.' I just thought that being a celebrity chef sounded better than working on a stall in Borough Market!
What do you cook at home and who do you cook for?
I cook for my family, for parties (my husband enjoys a good party, we love entertaining). I cook a lot of Scandinavian dishes and I like to experiment.
What is your favourite meal?
My favourite meal is fettuccini with white truffle and a little butter and black pepper, I just love it! And I love Muscat grapes if I want something sweet.
What are your aspirations in the world of cooking and food?
I was disappointed not to get through to the next round of Masterchef. I would love to be a TV presenter. In the meantime, I'm going to open a restaurant in Borough Market and take on a Swedish chef – I'm going to decorate it and contribute a lot of my ideas. It's my baby, it's going to happen.

Name: Daksha Mistry
Age: 45
Occupation: Trying to be a chef! At the moment, I cook for friends and family.
Place of residence: London
Why did you apply to Masterchef?
It was a really good opportunity and I thought, 'If I don't try, I don't know where I'll be.' My husband really encouraged me: he said it was an opportunity knocking, so I applied on the Internet. I went on Masterchef to show people that Indian food is not about the chicken tikka masala, korma and vindaloo that you get in Indian restaurants in the UK – these dishes don't even exist in India.
What do you cook at home and who do you cook for?
I cook for friends and family, sometimes up to 100 people! I cook whatever they want – all Indian food, of course.
What is your favourite meal?
My favourite is actually my own version of Italian food! It's a fusion of Italian and Indian: I make a pasta dish with puréed aubergine with basil, coriander, cumin, garlic and ginger poured over the pasta – that's my favourite.
What are your aspirations in the world of cooking and food?
My aim is to do a cookery show on television, to show people how to cook in the style of my region of India (Gujarat). I specialize in this cooking and I speak Gujarati. I'm convinced that one day I will do this.

Name: Katherine Haworth
Age: 47
Occupation: Freelance housekeeper and amateur cook.
Place of residence: Nineteen miles north of York
Why did you apply to Masterchef?
Because I really wanted to do something with my cooking, take it further and show the world I could cook, and then hopefully get some work as a cook.
What do you cook at home and who do you cook for?
I cook for my husband, my friends and my relatives. I cook absolutely everything. I particularly love Italian and Moroccan flavours. The only thing I never, ever cook is tripe (I even occasionally cook liver for the dog!).
What is your favourite meal?
I've got so many – it depends on the time of year. My absolute favourite is the simplest thing you could possibly think of: half a dozen oysters, some top-quality smoked salmon with some caviar, followed by a crème brûlée and accompanied by a bottle of the best bubbly. That's what we have for a real celebration.
What are your aspirations in the world of cooking and food?
I'd really love to be a recipe developer, or run a small, high-quality guest house.

Fish and Shel...

Fillet of Sea Trout on Asian Leaves

Wonderfully fresh salads such as this one are the base of a great many Asian dishes. It's a good one to keep in mind to use not only with fish but also with shellfish, such as prawns or roast lobster.

- → A LARGE BUNCH OF CORIANDER
- → A SMALL BUNCH OF MINT
- → 16 CHERRY TOMATOES, QUARTERED
- → 2 SHALLOTS, THINLY SLICED
- → 2 TSP PLAIN FLOUR
- → 4 X 150G (5OZ) THICK FILLETS OF SEA TROUT, SKIN ON (USE TAIL END OF SALMON IF SEA TROUT IS NOT AVAILABLE)
- → 2 TBSP VEGETABLE OIL
- → SEA SALT

For the dressing:
- → 1 LONG RED CHILLI, DESEEDED AND CHOPPED
- → 2 TSP CASTER SUGAR
- → 1 TBSP LIME JUICE
- → 2 TSP SESAME OIL
- → 2 TSP THAI FISH SAUCE (*NAM PLA*)

ⓜ MASTERCHEF TOP TIP

When cooking an oily pink fish such as trout or salmon, dry the skin well before placing it in the hot pan. Do not shake the pan during cooking or the flesh will tear from the skin. Leave the fish to cook over a high heat for a good 3 minutes, until the edges of the skin begin to brown and the fish can be easily lifted away from the hot surface.

John Torode, Masterchef Judge

1 First prepare the dressing. Pound the red chilli and sugar to a paste in a pestle and mortar. Add the lime juice, sesame oil and fish sauce and mix together well. The dressing should taste sweet, sour, salty and hot. Adjust the balance of ingredients, if necessary.

2 Roughly tear the coriander and mint leaves and mix them with the tomatoes and shallots. Chill until ready to serve.

3 Season the flour with a little sea salt and lightly dust the trout fillets in it.

4 Place a large, heavy-based frying pan over a high heat. When the pan is hot, add the vegetable oil. Place the fish fillets in the pan skin-side down and cook for about 3 minutes, until golden and crisp. Turn the fish over and cook for a further 2–3 minutes, until the flesh is opaque and firm to the touch. Remove from the heat.

5 Toss a little of the dressing with the salad. Arrange the salad on 4 plates and place the trout fillets on top. Drizzle with a little more dressing and serve immediately.

Masterchef Masterclass
John Torode's Flat Fish

First, a few fish facts. Like most produce, fish are seasonal. In general, they are best in the winter months, after they have had time to recover from the spawning season. They fall into two main categories – flat and round – and are further categorised by the type of water they come from: deep, shallow, cold or warm.

Flat fish live on the bottom of the ocean and bury themselves in the sand, camouflaged against predators, awaiting their prey. They are mostly thin, so the smaller ones should, if possible, be cooked on the bone, which will conduct the heat from the inside, helping the delicate flesh to cook more quickly and stay moist.

Round fish, such as cod, salmon, sea bass, haddock and hake, are very active, searching the seas for food and swimming huge distances to mate and spawn. Because of this they grow at a faster rate than flat fish and have large hunks of delicious, dense flesh, fantastic for fillets or steaks.

Many of the best-known flat fish – sole, plaice, turbot, skate and brill – are indigenous to UK waters, yet as a rule people aren't very confident about choosing and preparing them. Here are some points to consider when buying fish.

→ Avoid pre-packaged fish, as there is usually a piece of absorbent paper in the bottom of the tray, which can suck the moisture from the flesh, leaving it dry and pappy.

→ Find a good local fishmonger, or get to know the staff on your supermarket fish counter and check that the fish hasn't been fresh-frozen, then defrosted. When a fish is frozen, the water cells expand, then when it is defrosted they collapse, forcing out the water, so that the cooked texture can be dry and chalky.

→ The best fish counters have whole fish on display, so you can check that the eyes are clear and shiny and the gills moist – it's much more difficult to judge the age and condition of fish that has already been cut into fillets or steaks. The skin should shimmer, but beware of any fish whose flesh has a rainbow hue. This shows that it is old – not off, but past its prime.

→ Look for line-caught fish where you can, as this is a way of protesting against the massive dredgers that rape the seas of all that lies in their way.

Masterchef Masterclass
John Torode's Mash

Mashed potato must surely be the ultimate comfort food. Really good mash has to be beaten and worked quite hard until it is creamy and peaky but still has the texture of a good floury potato. If possible, buy potatoes that are covered in protective earth and quite fresh out of the ground. As potatoes get older, the starch begins to break down into sugar, so that you end up with a sweetish, sloppy, more cornflour-textured mash. The best varieties to use are large, floury ones such as Maris Piper, Desiree and Golden Wonder.

You can't really make hard and fast rules about the ratio of liquid or butter to potato. You need to take a look at the texture of your cooked potato and feel your way. It also depends on personal taste and how you plan to serve your mash. To cover a fish pie, it needs to be fairly stiff, whereas as an accompaniment to meat or fish you might want a more luxurious mash that is almost a purée.

There are many theories about how to cook mash but here are a few general principles.

→ Cut the peeled potatoes into even-sized chunks, so that they all cook at the same rate.
→ Put the potatoes in a pan of cold water and bring to the boil, rather than adding them to boiling water; this way, they are less likely to break up.
→ After draining the cooked potatoes, let them steam over the heat for a few minutes so the moisture evaporates.
→ Mash the potatoes until they are smooth and lump-free, then beat them vigorously to give them a light, fluffy texture. Don't use a food processor for this, though, as it makes them gluey.
→ Always serve mashed potato piping hot.

John Torode's
Basic Mash

SERVES 4–6
→ 2KG (4½LB) FLOURY POTATOES
→ ABOUT 100G (4OZ) BUTTER
→ ABOUT 200ML (7FL OZ) HOT MILK
→ 100ML (3½FL OZ) DOUBLE CREAM
   (OPTIONAL)
→ SEA SALT AND WHITE PEPPER

1 Peel the potatoes and cut them into even-sized chunks. Place them in a large pan of cold water, add a good handful of sea salt and bring to the boil.

2 Reduce the heat to a gentle simmer, so the water is just moving. Cook until you can easily slip a knife through a potato.

3 Drain the potatoes well in a sieve or colander, then return them to the pan. Place over a very low heat for a minute or two, shaking the pan occasionally, to steam off the excess moisture.

4 Mash with a potato masher or a fork (I prefer a fork). Alternatively pass the potatoes through a potato ricer or sieve. Keep the pan on the heat to evaporate any more moisture that comes from the potatoes as they are mashed.

5 Season well, add the butter and mix it in roughly. Then raise the heat a little and gradually add the milk, beating constantly with a wooden spoon. Work the potato, still on the hob, adding more milk and butter as you like, until the mixture becomes volcanic and starts erupting in bubbles. Add the cream, if using, then taste and adjust the seasoning.

6 Serve straight away, with something equally simple and equally sublime, such as a good piece of roast cod.

Fish Pie with Green Beans

There are fish pies and then there are fish pies! The important thing is that the pie should be moreish and comforting as well as being seasoned on all levels. Often people don't get the proportions correct, such as the ratio of mashed potato to sauce to fish. Many fish pies are made too heavy by the inclusion of a flour-based sauce, but not this one. This recipe could be renamed very, very good fish pie!

→ 675G (1½LB) FLOURY POTATOES, SUCH AS MARIS PIPER, PEELED AND CUT INTO CHUNKS
→ 40G (1½OZ) BUTTER
→ 350ML (12FL OZ) DOUBLE CREAM
→ 2 TBSP OLIVE OIL
→ 1 ONION, FINELY CHOPPED
→ 175G (6OZ) MATURE CHEDDAR CHEESE, GRATED
→ 1 HEAPED TSP MUSTARD POWDER
→ 2–3 TBSP CHOPPED PARSLEY
→ 2 TBSP LEMON JUICE
→ 450G (1LB) THICK SKINLESS COD FILLET
→ 16 RAW TIGER PRAWNS, PEELED
→ 175G (6OZ) FINE GREEN BEANS, TRIMMED
→ SALT AND WHITE PEPPER

1 Preheat the oven to 200°C/400°F/Gas Mark 6.

2 Cook the potatoes in boiling salted water until tender, then drain. Mash well and stir in half the butter and 3 tablespoons of the cream. Season to taste.

3 Heat the remaining butter and half the oil in a small saucepan. Add the onion and fry until soft and translucent. Stir in the remaining cream and bring to the boil, then remove from the heat. Stir in the cheese, mustard, parsley and lemon juice.

4 Slice the cod into meaty chunks and arrange them in a pan in a single layer. Add 100ml (3½fl oz) water, bring to a simmer, then cover and cook for 2–3 minutes, to firm up the fish. Drain well and arrange in an ovenproof serving dish with the prawns.

5 Pour the sauce over the fish. Spoon the potato on top and bake for 30 minutes, until piping hot and golden brown.

6 Put the green beans in a shallow ovenproof dish, coat with the remaining olive oil and season. Bake in the oven with the fish pie for the last 8–10 minutes of cooking time. Drain the oil from the beans and serve them with the fish pie.

Name: Christopher Souto
Age: 33
Occupation: Freelance IT Project Manager.
Place of residence: London
Why did you apply to Masterchef?
I wanted to explore my love of food and see if I had the creativity required to produce great meals.
What do you cook at home and who do you cook for?
Up until recently I didn't cook anything at home except fry-ups and the occasional Sunday roast. Now I will cook anything – fresh pastas, home-made soups, ethnic food, anything – the imagination is the only limit. I mainly cook for friends and my son.
What is your favourite meal?
I love Indian food. But any meal in good company is fantastic.
What are your aspirations in the world of cooking and food?
I would like to open a restaurant in southern Spain.

Name: Caroline Brewester
Age: 38
Occupation: Stockbroker for the last 15 years.
Place of residence: North London
Why did you apply to Masterchef?
I had taken a year out from broking and I'm interested in doing more food stuff. I saw an advert, and I would love to be a food writer so I thought this would be a way of pursuing that.
What do you cook at home and who do you cook for?
I cook all sorts of things, but most of what I cook has to be ready in about half an hour because of the hours I work, so I'm particularly fond of quick and easy recipes to cook at home: mostly English, Italian and North African food. I still have to learn more about Asian cookery. I cook for my husband, who's both my greatest fan and fiercest critic, and friends as well.
What is your favourite meal?
I'm too greedy to have one favourite!
What are your aspirations in the world of cooking and food?
To be a food writer, to show people it really is possible to cook at home and you don't need to aspire to be a chef to do so. There are really simple recipes you can make to impress your friends and your husband and to be a great home cook.

Name: Mark Todd
Age: 25
Occupation: I work for a publishing house as an advertising sales account manager.
Place of residence: Bath (but I'm from Darlington originally)
Why did you apply to Masterchef?
Because I fancied myself as a good cook! My friends told me to go for it, because I cook for them. It was a Friday afternoon at work, I had nothing better to do, so I filled in the application form.
What do you cook at home and who do you cook for?
I cook for anyone who comes to my house, mainly for my fiancée Esther, but also for dinner parties and when I go home to my family (apart from on Sundays when Mum cooks the roast). I like to experiment with different flavours, different produce.
What is your favourite meal?
Kerala chicken with pilau rice is my signature dish at home. I serve it with homemade tarka dal.
What are your aspirations in the world of cooking and food?
I want to own and run a restaurant. I've always wanted to. I want to be sat at the bar all night, with a glass of red wine, in my own restaurant by the time I'm 30.

Masterchef Masterclass
John Torode's Chips

In the UK 38,000 tonnes of potatoes per week are made into chips – which means that one in every four potatoes ends its life as a chip. Everyone loves them. We guard our own plateful fiercely, slapping would-be chip thieves' hands away with the cry, 'Get off my chips!' So why are they so popular? And what makes the perfect chip?

First of all, it has to be made from the right kind of potato – large, floury ones, such as Desiree, Pentland, Cyprus or Maris Piper. These will all produce chips that are crisp on the outside and fluffy in the centre. The potatoes should be covered with a good layer of protective dirt when you buy them – they keep better this way. They should not have been stored too long before use, otherwise their starch reverts to sugar and you won't get that lovely, fluffy interior. Although we tend not to think of potatoes as a seasonal item any more, the large English varieties are at their best for frying from late autumn to late spring.

Chips come in all shapes and sizes: from wafer-thin crisps and game chips to slender French fries, chunky chip-shop chips and crinkle-cut versions. The basic cooking method is the same for all of them. Here are some pointers for success:

→ Use an electric deep-fat fryer or a large, deep saucepan for frying chips. For safety reasons, never leave it unattended while cooking, and make sure the oil doesn't overheat (an electric fryer has a built-in thermostat; otherwise you can use a thermometer).
→ Before cooking, wash the chips in cold water to remove some of the starch, then dry them thoroughly to prevent splattering when you put them in the hot fat.
→ Use a generous quantity of clean oil and cook the chips in small batches, otherwise when you add the chips to the oil the temperature will drop dramatically, resulting in soggy chips. I recommend 2 litres (3½ pints) of oil to 300g (11oz) potatoes.
→ Fry the chips twice: once at a low temperature to cook them through and ensure tenderness, then again at a higher temperature so they become crisp and golden. This is the method used by chippies and restaurants across the country.
→ Drain the chips well on kitchen paper after frying, so they won't be greasy.

John Torode's
Big Chips

SERVES 4
→ 6 LARGE, FLOURY POTATOES
→ SUNFLOWER OR GROUNDNUT OIL
  FOR DEEP-FRYING
→ SALT

VARIATIONS
→ **French fries**
To make French fries, cut the potatoes into chips 8mm wide and about 5cm long. Soak them in cold water 3 or 4 times, then follow the instructions above, reducing the time for each frying to about 3 minutes.

→ **Crisps**
To make crisps at home, it is useful to have a mandoline or a food processor with a slicing attachment. Peel the potatoes and slice them to credit-card thickness – if you hold a slice up to the light you should almost be able to see through it. Place the slices in a sinkful of cold water and run the water over the top of them, stirring them about until the water is clear. This washes out all the excess starch so they become very crisp. Heat the oil to 190°C/375°F, using 2 litres of oil to 100g (4oz) of crisps. Gently place each slice in the oil as if you were the dealer at a card game. Cook for 3 minutes, stirring occasionally to prevent them sticking together (if they do stick, either the oil isn't hot enough or the potatoes have not been washed of all their starch). Cook for another 6 minutes or so, until they are well browned and crisp, then remove from the oil and place on kitchen paper to drain. Place in a brown paper bag while still warm and sprinkle with salt.

1 Peel the potatoes and cut them into chips 3cm (1¼ in) wide. Fill the sink with cold water, add the chips and leave them to soak for 5 minutes. Change the water and leave for a further 5 minutes. Drain well, then place the chips on a clean tea towel and pat dry.

2 Heat the oil to 140°C/275°F in a deep-fat fryer or a large, deep saucepan. Lower a small batch of chips into the oil in a chip basket and cook for 8–10 minutes, until the chips are soft and flaccid but still pale. Lift the basket out of the oil and drain, then spread the chips out on a tray lined with kitchen paper. Repeat with the remaining chips. This initial frying can be done several hours in advance. Once the chips are cold, you can store them in the fridge, which will make the insides even fluffier.

3 The final frying should be quite quick and the oil must be hot. The quantity of chips in the oil will determine how quickly it returns to the temperature you require so the outside is sealed and begins to brown. Heat the oil to 190°C/375°F and lower a small batch of chips into it. Leave to cook for 2 minutes, then give them a little shake. Cook for a further 4–5 minutes, until they are well coloured and crisp. Remove from the oil and leave to drain for a few minutes, then place in a bowl and sprinkle with salt.

Monkfish in Parma Ham with Chilli Beurre Blanc, Brussels Sprout Purée and Potato Waffles

This is a classic idea given a Masterchef twist with the addition of the punchy chilli beurre blanc. You could call it a new take on fish, chips and mushy peas. Monkfish is a great fish when fresh but if old and tired the flesh can become woolly when cooked, so make sure you buy yours from a good fishmonger.

→ 6–8 SLICES OF PARMA HAM (NOT TOO THIN)
→ 500G (1LB 2OZ) MONKFISH TAIL, DIVIDED INTO 2 FILLETS
→ 25G (1OZ) CLARIFIED BUTTER
→ SALT AND FRESHLY GROUND BLACK PEPPER

For the Brussels sprout purée:
→ 300G (11 OZ) BRUSSELS SPROUTS, TRIMMED AND HALVED
→ 25G (1OZ) BUTTER
→ 4–6 TBSP DOUBLE CREAM

For the potato waffles:
→ 2 LARGE WHITE POTATOES (ABOUT 300G/11OZ EACH), PEELED
→ 1 LITRE (1¾ PINTS) GROUNDNUT OIL

For the chilli beurre blanc:
→ 2 MILD LONG RED CHILLIES
→ 150G (5OZ) BUTTER
→ 20G (¾OZ) SHALLOT, FINELY CHOPPED
→ 1 TBSP WHITE WINE VINEGAR
→ 85ML (3FL OZ) DRY WHITE WINE
→ 85ML (3FL OZ) FISH STOCK
→ 1 TBSP DOUBLE CREAM
→ SALT AND WHITE PEPPER

1 Lay the Parma ham slices on a length of cling film, slightly overlapping them. Season the monkfish fillets with pepper and place them one on top of the other, thin end to thick end, to form an even cylinder. Then place them on the ham and roll up, using the cling film to help. Tuck in the ends of the ham. Wrap tightly in the cling film and chill for 1 hour.

2 Meanwhile, make the sprout purée. Cook the sprouts in boiling salted water for 3–4 minutes, until just tender. Drain well, place in a food processor and blend to a chunky purée. Add the butter, 4 tablespoons of the cream and some pepper. Blend again to purée, adding more cream if necessary for a looser texture. Spoon the purée into a small saucepan and set aside.

3 Cut the potatoes into waffle slices using the waffle attachment of a mandoline. Put them in a large bowl of cold water. Pour the groundnut oil into a large frying pan to a depth of about 6cm (2½ in) and heat to 160°C/325°F.

4 Drain the potato slices, dry them well on kitchen paper and test the oil by dropping a slice of potato into it. It should brown in about a minute. Fry the potato slices in batches, removing them with a slotted spoon when done and leaving to drain on baking trays lined with kitchen paper.

5 For the chilli sauce, cut the chillies lengthways in half, remove the seeds and set them aside. Finely dice 1 chilli, then roughly chop the other one and set it aside with the chilli seeds.

6 Melt 15g (½oz) of the butter in a small, heavy-based saucepan (dice the remaining butter and chill it). Add the shallot to the pan

'Caroline has a good understanding of ingredients and the way they marry together.'
Peter Richards, Chef Mentor

and fry gently until translucent. Add the chilli seeds, roughly chopped chilli and the white wine vinegar. Simmer until reduced by two-thirds. Pour in the white wine and reduce again by two-thirds, then add the fish stock and reduce by two-thirds a final time. Strain the reduction into a clean saucepan and set aside.

7 To cook the fish, preheat the oven to 200°C/400°F/Gas Mark 6. Heat a heavy-based non-stick frying pan until very hot and add the clarified butter. Remove the cling film from the fish and brown it on all sides in the butter. Transfer to a baking sheet lined with baking parchment and bake for 8–10 minutes. Remove from the oven and leave to rest in a warm place for 6–7 minutes.

8 To finish the sauce, reheat the reduction in the pan, then stir in the cream. Whisk in the chilled diced butter a little at a time over a medium heat. Season to taste with salt and white pepper, then stir in the finely diced chilli.

9 Just before serving, gently reheat the Brussels sprout purée. Place the trays of potato waffles in the oven for a couple of minutes to heat through and crisp up, then sprinkle them with a little salt.

10 Slice the monkfish into 4 and put it on to 4 warmed plates with a spoonful of the Brussels sprout purée and a pile of waffles. Drizzle a little of the chilli beurre blanc over the fish and serve the rest separately.

Marinated Seared Tuna on a Garlic and Anchovy Croûton with Creamed Fennel and French Beans Provençal

Katherine's inspired recipe evokes the flavours of the Mediterranean. The tuna, anchovies and beans immediately suggest a classic salad niçoise, but the creamy fennel adds a different texture, binding the dish into a coherent whole.

→ 4 X 175G (6OZ) TUNA STEAKS, ABOUT 2.5CM (1 IN) THICK
→ 100ML (3½FL OZ) WHITE WINE
→ 15G (½OZ) BUTTER
→ 1 FENNEL BULB, THINLY SLICED
→ OLIVE OIL FOR BRUSHING
→ SALT AND FRESHLY GROUND BLACK PEPPER

For the marinade:
→ 1 TSP FENNEL SEEDS
→ JUICE OF 1 LIME
→ 2 TBSP LIGHT SOY SAUCE
→ 1 TBSP OLIVE OIL

For the garlic and anchovy croûtons:
→ 2 TBSP OLIVE OIL
→ 75G (3OZ) BUTTER
→ 4 SLICES OF GOOD-QUALITY WHITE BREAD
→ 4 ANCHOVY FILLETS IN OLIVE OIL
→ 3 GARLIC CLOVES, CRUSHED

For the French beans Provençal:
→ 150G (5OZ) FRENCH BEANS, TRIMMED
→ 1 TBSP OLIVE OIL
→ 1 GARLIC CLOVE, CRUSHED
→ 2 TBSP TOMATO PURÉE
→ ½ TSP VERJUICE
→ 2-3 SUN-DRIED TOMATOES IN OLIVE OIL, FINELY CHOPPED
→ ½ RED PEPPER, ROASTED, PEELED AND FINELY SLICED
→ 50G (2OZ) GREEN OLIVES, SLICED

MASTERCHEF TOP TIP
Verjuice – or verjus, to give it its French name – is the juice of unripe white grapes and has a fresh but acidic taste. You only need a small amount, so use it judiciously.
Peter Richards, Masterchef Mentor

1 Mix all the marinade ingredients together in a shallow, non-metallic dish and season to taste. Lay the tuna in the dish and turn until thoroughly coated in the marinade.

2 For the fennel, bring the wine and butter to the boil in a small pan. Add the fennel and some seasoning and cook over a medium heat for 15 minutes, until the fennel is soft and creamy and the liquid has evaporated. Remove from the heat and keep warm.

3 For the croûtons, heat half the olive oil and butter in a large frying pan, add 2 slices of bread and fry until golden on both sides. Remove from the pan and repeat with the remaining bread, oil and butter. Cut off the crusts to make pieces a similar size to the tuna steaks. Place on kitchen paper to absorb excess oil. Dry the anchovy fillets on kitchen paper and mash with the garlic to make a paste. Spread the paste over the fried bread and set aside.

4 For the French beans, bring a saucepan of lightly salted water to the boil and cook the beans for 3–4 minutes, until just tender. Drain, then cool under cold running water. Warm the olive oil in a pan and add the garlic. Cook for a few seconds, then add the tomato purée, verjuice and some salt and pepper. Cook gently for 2–3 minutes, then stir in the sun-dried tomatoes, red pepper, olives and green beans. Warm through, then set aside.

5 Preheat the oven to 190°C/375°F/Gas Mark 5. Heat a ridged griddle pan and brush with oil. Wipe the tuna dry on kitchen paper and brush with a little olive oil. Lay the tuna on the hot griddle and sear for about 2–3 minutes on each side, until lightly caramelised on the outside but still pink in the middle. While the tuna is cooking, put the croûtons in the oven to warm through.

6 Put a croûton on each serving plate. Top with a tuna steak and some creamed fennel and serve with the French beans.

Sea Bass with Anchovy Sauce, Spinach and Cannellini Beans

The River Café in London has been using the combination of sea bass and anchovies for as long as I can remember. The anchovies provide the saltiness that is needed to make the sea bass stand out as one of the greatest all-round fish. Bolstered by pancetta and cannellini beans, this will make a great addition to your winter repertoire.

→ 100G (4OZ) PANCETTA, FINELY DICED
→ 400G (14OZ) TIN OF CANNELLINI BEANS, DRAINED AND RINSED
→ 2 HEAPED TBSP FINELY CHOPPED FLAT-LEAF PARSLEY
→ 1 TBSP FINELY CHOPPED MINT
→ 3 GARLIC CLOVES, FINELY CHOPPED
→ JUICE OF 1 LEMON
→ 2–3 TBSP OLIVE OIL
→ 2 TBSP PLAIN FLOUR
→ 1 TSP SEA SALT
→ 4 X 200G (7OZ) SEA BASS FILLETS, SKIN ON
→ 50G (2OZ) BUTTER
→ 200G (7OZ) BABY SPINACH
→ 5 ANCHOVY FILLETS IN EXTRA VIRGIN OLIVE OIL, FINELY CHOPPED, PLUS 2 TSP OF THEIR OIL
→ 1 TSP CHOPPED THYME
→ 4 TBSP DRY SHERRY
→ FRESHLY GROUND BLACK PEPPER

1 Preheat the oven to 200°C/400°F/Gas Mark 6.

2 In a frying pan, slowly cook the pancetta until it is beginning to crisp up. Stir in the cannellini beans and heat through. Add the parsley, mint, half the garlic and the lemon juice. Season with plenty of black pepper and drizzle a little of the olive oil over the top, then cover and keep warm.

3 Mix the flour and sea salt together on a plate and lightly dust the skin side of the fish fillets, tapping off any excess flour.

4 Heat a little of the olive oil in a large ovenproof frying pan. Place the fillets in the pan, skin-side down, and cook over a high heat for 5 minutes to crisp the skin. Transfer the pan to the oven and cook for 4–5 minutes, until the fish is just done. Do not turn the fish over.

5 Put half the butter in a saucepan with 1 tablespoon of water and bring to the boil. Stir in the spinach, then cover the pan and cook for 1 minute, until the spinach has wilted. Remove from the heat and keep warm. Drain off any excess liquid before serving.

6 In a small saucepan, heat the 2 teaspoons of anchovy oil, add the remaining garlic and the anchovies and cook over a low heat, stirring, for about 2 minutes, until the garlic is soft. Add the thyme and sherry and warm through. Remove from the heat and whisk in the remaining butter.

7 Pile up the spinach in the centre of 4 warm serving plates. Place the fish fillets on top of the spinach. Spoon the pancetta and beans around the outside and drizzle the anchovy sauce over the fish. Serve immediately.

Meat, Poultry and Game

Stuffed Chicken Parma Parcels

When Scott made these parcels he said that he wanted them to resemble little hams, and strangely enough they do! The boned chicken legs must have the skin removed or the ham will not stick to the meat. Use good-quality dried porcini mushrooms for the best flavour and make sure they are reconstituted properly, as they can be tough if not allowed to soak for long enough.

→ 4 CHICKEN LEGS, SKINNED AND BONED
→ 50G (2OZ) DRIED PORCINI MUSHROOMS
→ 2 SHALLOTS, FINELY CHOPPED
→ 50G (2OZ) BUTTER
→ 2 GARLIC CLOVES, CRUSHED
→ 150G (5OZ) BABY SPINACH
→ 100G (4OZ) MOZZARELLA CHEESE, GRATED
→ 250G (9OZ) RICOTTA CHEESE
→ 8 SLICES OF PARMA HAM
→ 3 TBSP OLIVE OIL
→ 1 TSP BALSAMIC VINEGAR
→ SALT AND FRESHLY GROUND BLACK PEPPER

MASTERCHEF TOP TIP

Boning a chicken leg is not difficult. Just follow the line of the bone with the tip of a sharp boning knife, gently scraping the meat away as you go. Remember that chicken bones are brittle. It is best to cut through the joints rather than chopping through bones, as they will chip and splinter.

Peter Richards, Masterchef Mentor

1 Preheat the oven to 200°C/400°F/Gas Mark 6.

2 Place the chicken meat between 2 layers of cling film. Flatten to an even thickness with a meat mallet or rolling pin, then set aside.

3 Put the dried porcini in a bowl and pour on 250ml (8fl oz) hot water. Leave for 30 minutes, then drain well, reserving the soaking liquor. Slice the mushrooms if large.

4 Fry the shallots in the butter until soft and translucent. Add the porcini and garlic and cook for 2 minutes. Stir in the spinach and cook until wilted. Remove from the heat and drain off any excess liquid.

5 Mix the grated mozzarella and ricotta together in a bowl and stir in the spinach mixture. Season to taste.

6 Lay 2 slices of Parma ham on a board, slightly overlapping. Place a flattened chicken leg on top. Spoon a quarter of the stuffing mixture into the middle of the leg and roll it up, with the Parma ham on the outside. Secure with a cocktail stick. Repeat with the remaining chicken legs. Chill for 30 minutes.

7 Heat the oil in an ovenproof frying pan and brown the stuffed chicken legs for 2–3 minutes on each side. Transfer the pan to the oven and cook, uncovered, for 20 minutes or until golden brown and cooked through. Remove from the oven and transfer the chicken to a plate, removing the cocktail sticks. Keep warm.

8 Pour the reserved porcini liquor into the pan and bring to the boil on the hob, scraping up any residue from the base of the pan with a wooden spoon. Simmer until reduced by half, then add the balsamic vinegar and cook for 1–2 minutes. Serve with the chicken.

Thai Green Chicken Curry

A well-made green curry is a wonderful thing. It needs punch but, more importantly, it also needs heat. After you've been handling chillies, remember to wash your hands – first in cold water, then with soap. If you use hot water first, you will open the pores and end up with painful hands.

→ 150ML (¼ PINT) COCONUT CREAM
→ 8 SKINLESS CHICKEN THIGHS, BONED AND CUT INTO 2CM (¾ IN) DICE
→ 400ML (14FL OZ) TIN OF COCONUT MILK
→ 2 KAFFIR LIME LEAVES
→ 1½ TBSP THAI FISH SAUCE (*NAM PLA*)
→ 1 TSP SUGAR
→ 150G (5OZ) AUBERGINE, CUT INTO BITE-SIZED PIECES
→ A HANDFUL OF BASIL LEAVES

For the green curry paste:
→ 1 TBSP CORIANDER SEEDS
→ 1 TSP CUMIN SEEDS
→ 15 GREEN BIRD'S EYE CHILLIES, CHOPPED
→ 3 TBSP FINELY CHOPPED SHALLOTS
→ 1 TBSP FINELY CHOPPED GARLIC
→ 1 TSP FINELY CHOPPED GALANGAL
→ 1 TBSP FINELY SLICED LEMONGRASS
→ 1 TSP FINELY CHOPPED KAFFIR LIME LEAVES
→ ½ TSP FINELY CHOPPED CORIANDER ROOT
→ 5 BLACK PEPPERCORNS
→ 1 TSP SALT
→ 1 TSP SHRIMP PASTE

1 For the curry paste, dry-fry the coriander and cumin seeds in a wok over a low heat for about 5 minutes, then grind to a powder in a pestle and mortar.

2 Put all the rest of the curry paste ingredients except the shrimp paste into a food processor and mix well. Add the ground roasted spices and the shrimp paste and blend to a fine-textured paste.

3 For the curry, heat the coconut cream in a wok until it begins to have an oily sheen. Add 3 level tablespoons of the green curry paste and stir well (the rest of the paste will keep in the fridge for about a week, or it can be frozen). Stir in the chicken and cook until it begins to brown.

4 Add the coconut milk, lime leaves, fish sauce and sugar and bring to the boil. Add the aubergine and simmer for about 20 minutes, until the chicken is cooked through.

5 Stir in the basil leaves. Remove from the heat and serve with fragrant jasmine rice or noodles.

MASTERCHEF TOP TIP
To make authentic Thai dishes, you need to get hold of genuine Thai ingredients. Nowadays most big cities have a Thai emporium, thanks to the rise in popularity of Thai restaurants. They usually have fresh imports delivered once or twice a week. Ask at your nearest Thai shop which days their produce arrives, and shop then.
Gregg Wallace, Masterchef Judge

Masterchef Masterclass
John Torode's coating and crumbing

I have always enjoyed food that has been cooked in some form of casing, whether it is breadcrumbs, egg or batter. There are several advantages. First, a delicate piece of fish, meat or even vegetable is well protected in this way, allowing it to be subject to high heat and cooked quickly. Secondly, the food remains tender and retains all its juices. And finally, you can use a more expensive cut without it losing volume during cooking, thus making it go further.

The principle is simple: the protective casing seals quickly when heat is applied, allowing the interior to steam. This reduces loss from evaporation and at the same time retains all the flavour and nutrients.

Below are some general guidelines for coating food before frying:
- → The pieces of food should be an even thickness. If coating uneven cuts of meat, such as chicken breasts, put them between two sheets of cling film and bat them out with a meat mallet or rolling pin.
- → Season your coating ingredients well with salt and pepper, plus any other flavourings you like, such as herbs, spices or cheese.
- → Coatings usually consist of flour, then beaten egg, and sometimes a final layer of breadcrumbs. Use just a light dusting of flour, then dip the food in the egg until thoroughly coated and let the excess drain off.
- → If adding a coating of breadcrumbs, spread these out in a shallow dish and press the food in them gently so it is covered in a thin, even layer. Then turn it over to coat the other side.
- → Shallow-fry the coated food in a generous amount of oil or butter, but not so much that the food is swimming in it.
- → Make sure the fat is sizzling hot (but not smoking hot) before adding the food. If it isn't hot enough, the coating will not seal quickly enough and will be soggy. If it is too hot, the coating will burn.

John Torode's
Veal Escalopes Coated with Egg and Parmesan

SERVES 4
- 4 VEAL ESCALOPES, WEIGHING ABOUT 120G (4½OZ) EACH
- 50G (2OZ) ROCKET
- 4 TBSP OLIVE OIL
- 4 TBSP VEGETABLE OIL
- 50G (2OZ) PLAIN FLOUR
- 50G (2OZ) BUTTER
- 2 TSP WHITE WINE VINEGAR
- FRESHLY GROUND BLACK PEPPER
- 1 LEMON, QUARTERED, TO SERVE

For the coating:
- 2 MEDIUM EGGS
- 4 ANCHOVIES, FINELY CHOPPED
- 175G (6OZ) PARMESAN CHEESE, FRESHLY GRATED
- 2 TBSP CHOPPED FLAT-LEAF PARSLEY
- ½ TSP FRESHLY GROUND BLACK PEPPER

Dipped in a light coating of egg and cheese, the veal in this recipe is substantial enough to be served with just some rocket salad to accompany it. It makes a good winter lunch or supper dish. Pork fillets can be used instead of veal.

1 Put the veal escalopes between 2 sheets of cling film and bat them out with a meat mallet or a rolling pin to about 1 cm (½ in) thick.

2 For the coating, put the eggs in a large bowl and whisk together for 1 minute, until light. Stir in the anchovies, Parmesan, parsley and black pepper.

3 Place the rocket in a shallow serving dish and dress with the olive oil and some black pepper, then set aside.

4 Heat a large, heavy-based frying pan over a high heat and add the vegetable oil.

5 Spread the flour out in a large, shallow dish and turn the veal escalopes in it until evenly coated. Then dip them in the egg mixture. Place the escalopes in the pan and cook for 1 minute. Reduce the heat to medium and cook for a further 2 minutes, until golden underneath.

6 Turn and cook the other side for 2–3 minutes, then add the butter to the pan. When it has melted, pour in the vinegar, tilting the pan to ensure the juices combine.

7 Remove the escalopes from the pan and lay them on the dressed rocket. Drizzle with the melted butter from the pan and serve with the lemon wedges.

Lamb Kofte with Fragrant Pilau Rice, Marinated Peppers and Tzatsiki

Some would call a variety of dishes on one plate a mezze, but in this case each one is essential to the success of the others. The kofte should be very well seasoned, as the rice can be a little sweet, so the meat and the tzatsiki are there to lift the dish.

→ 2 TSP CUMIN SEEDS
→ 2 TBSP CORIANDER SEEDS
→ 500G (1LB 2OZ) MINCED LAMB
→ JUICE OF 2 LEMONS
→ 4 TBSP CHOPPED MINT
→ 1 LARGE EGG, LIGHTLY BEATEN
→ 2 RED PEPPERS, HALVED AND DESEEDED
→ 2 GREEN PEPPERS, HALVED AND DESEEDED
→ 3 TBSP OLIVE OIL
→ SALT AND FRESHLY GROUND BLACK PEPPER
For the pilau rice:
→ 2 TBSP OLIVE OIL
→ 1 ONION, FINELY CHOPPED
→ 40G (1½OZ) PINE NUTS
→ 40G (1½OZ) CURRANTS
→ 1 CINNAMON STICK, HALVED
→ 1 GARLIC CLOVE, CRUSHED
→ 150G (5OZ) BASMATI RICE, RINSED WELL
→ 350ML (12FL OZ) VEGETABLE STOCK
For the tzatsiki:
→ 2 GARLIC CLOVES, PEELED
→ 150G (5OZ) PLAIN YOGHURT
→ 1 TBSP CHOPPED MINT

1 Preheat the oven to 220°C/425°F/Gas Mark 7.

2 Place the cumin and coriander seeds in a hot, dry frying pan and roast for 1–2 minutes. Crush in a pestle and mortar and set aside.

3 Put the lamb into a bowl and stir in half the lemon juice, plus the mint, crushed cumin and coriander. Season well. Bind with the egg and shape into 8 patties. Chill for 30 minutes.

4 Place the peppers on a baking tray and roast in the preheated oven for 20–30 minutes, until blackened and blistered. Put them in a bowl, cover with cling film and leave for 10 minutes, then peel off the skins. Slice the peppers thinly. Put them in a dish, toss with the remaining lemon juice and set aside.

5 For the rice, heat the olive oil in a large saucepan, add the onion and fry for 4–5 minutes, until golden. Stir in the pine nuts, currants, cinnamon and garlic and cook for 2 minutes, stirring constantly. Add the rice to the pan, stirring until well coated in the oil, and cook for 2 minutes. Add the stock and ½ teaspoon of salt. Stir once and cover with a tight-fitting lid, then reduce the heat to very low and cook for 15 minutes. All the liquid should have been absorbed and the rice should be fluffy and perfectly cooked.

6 To make the tzatsiki, put the garlic cloves into a pestle and mortar with a little salt and crush to a paste. Put the yoghurt into a small bowl and stir in the garlic and mint.

7 Next, cook the kofte. Heat the olive oil in a large frying pan, add the lamb patties and cook for about 5 minutes on each side, turning occasionally, until golden brown and cooked through.

8 Pile the rice on a large serving plate. Arrange the peppers in a line down the centre of the rice and top with the kofte, drizzled with a little tzatsiki. Serve the remaining tzatsiki separately.

Lamb with Minted Lime Salsa and Chilli Roasted Vegetables

Many people associate eating lamb with Easter, but later-season lamb (say, late September) has a far superior flavour. The minted lime salsa gives the lamb the moisture it needs. The dish could also cope with a good blob of aïoli, or garlic mayonnaise (see page 118).

Remember to keep the lamb pink, as the more it is cooked, the drier it becomes (this doesn't apply, of course, if you are cooking it slowly in liquid – when making a stew, for example).

→ 2 SWEET POTATOES, PEELED AND CUT INTO CHUNKS
→ 4 SMALL MARIS PIPER POTATOES, PEELED AND HALVED
→ 2 PARSNIPS, CUT INTO CHUNKS
→ 1 RED ONION, SLICED INTO WEDGES
→ 1 GARLIC BULB, CUT HORIZONTALLY IN HALF
→ 5 TBSP OLIVE OIL
→ 1 MILD RED CHILLI, DESEEDED AND CHOPPED
→ 1 MILD GREEN CHILLI, DESEEDED AND CHOPPED
→ 8 LAMB LOIN CHOPS
→ SALT AND FRESHLY GROUND BLACK PEPPER

For the minted lime salsa:
→ 2 TBSP OLIVE OIL
→ 2 SHALLOTS, FINELY DICED
→ 2 TSP GRATED FRESH GINGER
→ 2 TBSP FINE-CUT LIME MARMALADE
→ JUICE AND GRATED ZEST OF 1 LIME
→ 2 TBSP CHOPPED MINT
→ 1 TBSP CHOPPED CORIANDER

1 Preheat the oven to 220°C/425°F/Gas Mark 7.

2 Put the potatoes, parsnips, red onion and garlic in a shallow baking dish. Drizzle 3 tablespoons of the olive oil over the vegetables and season with salt and pepper. Place in the oven and roast for 30 minutes. Stir in the chillies 5 minutes before the end of cooking.

3 For the salsa, mix all the ingredients together and set aside.

4 Heat the remaining olive oil in a heavy-based frying pan. Season the lamb chops, add to the pan and sear for 5–6 minutes on each side (you will need to cook them in batches). Cover and keep warm.

5 Arrange the roasted vegetables and lamb chops in a serving dish. Spoon the minted lime salsa over the chops and serve.

Inspired by contestant Karen Gemmel

Minted Lamb and Rosemary Kebabs with Roasted Vegetables

Lamb and rosemary, what can you say? What a classic, and then served with mint sauce – wow! An underrated cut of meat, lamb neck fillets are tender and full of flavour. Ask your butcher to remove most of the fat, or slip a sharp knife under the fat and gently slide the blade from one end to the other. The meat is delicate and will cook very quickly, so prepare all the rest of the ingredients before cooking the kebabs.

→ 5 SMALL, FLOURY POTATOES, SUCH AS MARIS PIPER, PEELED AND CUT INTO GOOD-SIZED CHUNKS
→ 1 RED PEPPER, HALVED AND DESEEDED
→ 1 GREEN PEPPER, HALVED AND DESEEDED
→ 1 RED ONION, ROUGHLY CHOPPED
→ 100ML (3½FL OZ) OLIVE OIL
→ 100G (4OZ) GREEN BEANS
→ 2 X 350G (12OZ) LAMB NECK FILLETS, CUT INTO 2CM (¾ IN) DICE
→ 8 LONG, WOODY ROSEMARY SPRIGS TO USE AS SKEWERS (OR 8 BAMBOO SKEWERS AND A FEW SPRIGS OF ROSEMARY)
→ 200ML (7FL OZ) RED WINE
→ 2 TSP MINT JELLY
→ SALT AND FRESHLY GROUND BLACK PEPPER

1 Preheat the oven to 220°C/425°F/Gas Mark 7.

2 Put the potatoes, peppers and onion in a roasting tin, pour in half the oil and toss to coat. Place in the oven and roast for 20 minutes.

3 Remove the vegetables from the oven. Put the peppers in a bowl and cover them with cling film for 10 minutes to loosen the skin. Skin the peppers and roughly chop them into chunks. Put to one side with the onion, cover and keep warm. Return the potatoes to the oven.

4 Blanch the green beans in boiling salted water for 1 minute, then drain, refresh in cold water and drain again. Set aside.

5 Skewer the lamb on to the 8 rosemary 'sticks' (or on to 8 bamboo skewers, placing the sprigs of rosemary between the meat) and season well. Heat the remaining oil in a large frying pan. Sear the skewered lamb for 4 minutes on each side, then transfer to the oven, placing it on top of the potatoes. Cook for 5 minutes.

6 Meanwhile, pour the red wine into the frying pan and cook over a high heat, scraping up any sediment from the base of the pan with a wooden spoon. Boil until the wine is reduced by half, then stir in the mint jelly. Transfer to a serving jug and keep warm.

7 Remove the roasting tin from the oven. Transfer the lamb kebabs to a plate and keep warm. Drain away any excess oil from the tin and stir in the peppers, onion and blanched green beans. Heat through for a couple of minutes in the oven.

8 Arrange the lamb kebabs on top of the roasted vegetables. Serve with the minted red wine sauce.

Masterchef Masterclass
John Torode's Roast Poultry

Roasting a bird or a joint of meat on a Sunday is a memory from a bygone era for many of us. Our lifestyles have changed so much that it is the sound of cash registers we hear now, rather than the sizzle of roasted meat. It is no longer the norm for the smell of crisp, well-seasoned meat, and potatoes, carrots and parsnips caramelising in the oven, to be wafting through the house as friends and family arrive for Sunday lunch. Maybe I can persuade you not to go shopping but to turn on the oven instead and get roasting.

A roast should be a treat, but you are not going to get the true taste of roast chicken (or duck, or turkey or any other fowl) unless you buy a decent bird. Never forget that if the bird has lived well, you will eat well. Freedom to roam and a diet based on grain are essential to the flavour, which means you need to buy at least a free-range bird, preferably an organic one. Free-range birds vary considerably in quality, from ones that have been kept in conditions that barely improve upon standard broiler houses to ones that have had the full run of the farmyard and been fed on maize. Organic birds are reared and fed according to strictly monitored welfare standards.

Once you've selected your bird, cooking it is comparatively simple, but there are a few general rules to observe:

→ Choose a roasting tin that is the correct size for your bird. There should be enough space around the bird for the juices to flow but not so much space that they will spread thinly and burn.

→ Most birds need some fat added before cooking, to keep them moist and help crisp up the skin. You can rub oil or butter over them, or lay strips of bacon over the top.

→ Season the bird well inside and out.

→ Make sure the oven is preheated to the correct temperature before putting the bird in.

→ Calculate an approximate cooking time before you put the bird in the oven. In general, a chicken will take 1–1¼ hours, a duck about 1½ hours and a turkey can take as long as 3 hours, depending on size.

→ To test whether the bird is done, insert a knife between the thigh and the breast; if the juices run clear rather than pink, it is ready.

→ Leave the bird to rest in a warm place for 10–15 minutes before serving. This results in tender, succulent meat.

Roast Duck with Red Wine and Sour Cherry Sauce and Sweet Potato Mash

Well, you really can't go wrong with this combination. It's a real crowd-pleaser for both Easter and Christmas. You may find it easier to serve it in the middle of the table and let everyone help themselves rather than as a plate of food, as it can look a little messy.

- 2–2.25KG (4½–5LB) GRESSINGHAM DUCK
- 150G (5OZ) DRIED SOUR CHERRIES
- 300ML (½ PINT) DRY RED WINE
- 50G (2OZ) GRANULATED SUGAR
- 2 TBSP GOOD-QUALITY RED WINE VINEGAR
- SEA SALT AND FRESHLY GROUND BLACK PEPPER

For the sweet potato mash:
- 2 SWEET POTATOES
- 1 SMALL SWEDE, CUT INTO CHUNKS
- A GOOD KNOB OF BUTTER
- 2 TBSP SINGLE CREAM

For the cabbage:
- 1 SAVOY CABBAGE, CORED AND FINELY SHREDDED
- 150G (5OZ) SMOKED STREAKY BACON, CUT INTO FINE STRIPS
- 15G (½OZ) BUTTER

1 Preheat the oven to 220°C/425°F/Gas Mark 7.

2 Trim and discard any loose fat from the duck cavity. Prick the duck all over with a sharp knife and sprinkle with sea salt, rubbing it into the skin. Season with black pepper. Place the duck on a rack in a roasting tin and roast for 20 minutes. Reduce the oven temperature to 200°C/400°F/Gas Mark 6 and cook the duck for about an hour longer, depending on size.

3 For the sauce, place the cherries, red wine, sugar and red wine vinegar in a pan and bring to a simmer. Reduce the heat to barely simmering and cook, uncovered, for 50 minutes–1 hour, stirring occasionally, until the sauce has reduced and thickened.

4 When the duck has about 45 minutes left to cook, prepare the mash. Put the unpeeled sweet potatoes on a tray in the oven with the duck and roast for 45 minutes, until tender. Cook the swede in boiling salted water until tender, then drain and return to the pan. Scoop out the soft flesh from the sweet potatoes, discarding the skin. Mash the swede and sweet potato together with the butter and cream. Heat through gently for a couple of minutes, then season with salt and plenty of black pepper. Keep warm.

5 To test if the duck is done, push a skewer into the thickest part of the flesh; if the juices run clear, it is ready. Remove from the oven, turn upside down and cover loosely with foil. Leave to rest.

6 Cook the shredded cabbage in a large pan of boiling salted water for 2–3 minutes, then drain and refresh in cold water. In a large frying pan, cook the bacon in the butter for 2–3 minutes. Stir in the cabbage, then cover and cook for 3 minutes, until the cabbage is tender but still has a little bite. Adjust the seasoning.

7 Transfer the duck to a serving platter and serve with the sour cherry sauce, sweet potato mash and cabbage.

Seared Duck Breast with Chilli Greens

Try to find a Barbary duck for this recipe – it's bigger and of superior quality. The slow cooking at the start of this recipe, where the fat is rendered from under the skin, is important: this fat is then used to baste the meat and keep it as moist as possible.

- → 4 DUCK BREASTS
- → LEAVES FROM 4 SPRIGS OF THYME
- → 2 TBSP RUNNY HONEY
- → 2 TBSP SOY SAUCE
- → 4 TBSP ORANGE JUICE
- → 4 TBSP WHITE WINE VINEGAR
- → 1 TSP CASTER SUGAR
- → 25G (1OZ) CLARIFIED BUTTER
- → SALT AND FRESHLY GROUND BLACK PEPPER

For the chilli greens:
- → 150G (5OZ) BROCCOLI
- → 100G (4OZ) FRENCH BEANS, TRIMMED
- → 1 PAK CHOY, CUT INTO QUARTERS
- → 1 TBSP GROUNDNUT OIL
- → 1 MILD LONG RED CHILLI, FINELY CHOPPED
- → 1 GARLIC CLOVE, FINELY CHOPPED

1 Preheat the oven to 200°C/400°F/Gas Mark 6.

2 Score the skin of the duck with a sharp knife. Put the duck breasts in a shallow dish and season with salt and pepper. Rub the thyme leaves, honey and soy sauce into the scored duck skin and leave to marinate for 10 minutes.

3 Mix the orange juice, vinegar and sugar together in a small jug and set aside.

4 Heat a large, heavy-based ovenproof frying pan over a medium heat and melt the butter in it. Place the duck breasts in the pan, skin-side down, and cook slowly for about 5 minutes, so the fat renders from under the skin and the skin becomes golden brown.

5 Turn the duck over and transfer the pan to the oven. Cook for 5–7 minutes, until the duck is cooked but still pink in the centre. Transfer the duck to a plate, cover and keep warm.

6 Strain off about half the fat from the frying pan. Add the orange juice mixture to the pan, together with any marinade, and place on the hob over a fairly high heat. Simmer until reduced by about half to a fairly thick syrup. Remove from the heat and keep warm.

7 Steam the vegetables over boiling water for about 3 minutes; they should remain slightly crisp. Meanwhile, heat the groundnut oil in a frying pan, add the chilli and garlic and fry for about 30 seconds, just to release their flavour. Add the steamed vegetables and stir-fry for 2–3 minutes in the chilli and garlic oil. Season to taste and remove from the heat.

8 Slice the duck breasts and pour any meat juices into the sauce. Reheat the sauce gently. Arrange the chilli greens and slices of duck on a plate and drizzle with a little of the sauce. Pour the remainder into a jug and serve immediately.

Masterchef Masterclass
John Torode's Burger

Burgers are so ubiquitous that you may wonder what is the point of making them at home. Well, the point is that they will be a lot better than most of the ones you can buy. And, of course, it means you can make them exactly to your liking.

The perfect burger should be big and juicy, even when cooked well done. To achieve this, you need to include fat in the mince. I like to use 40 per cent fat, which I know sounds a lot but it effectively bastes the meat during cooking, ensuring it stays moist. Most of it will drain off, leaving you with a succulent, well-flavoured but not overly fatty burger.

The meat for burgers should be coarsely minced. Most butchers mince their meat on a medium setting, so you may have to ask to have yours done separately. Or you can mince it yourself at home if you have a mincer. Chuck, skirt and rump are all good choices but remember to ask the butcher to include some fat.

I have another little secret when it comes to burgers. Instead of salt I use oyster sauce to season the meat. I find salt can make the mixture dry and crumbly because it draws out water, whereas if you use oyster sauce the meat stays moist and binds together well.

To get the best results, follow the tips below:
→ Use meat straight from the fridge and make sure it is well chilled. This will help it to bind together.
→ Mix everything together as quickly and lightly as possible, preferably with your hands.
→ Dampen your hands slightly before shaping the burgers, so that the mixture doesn't stick to them.
→ Cook the burgers in a very hot, heavy-based pan and resist the temptation to move them about before they have formed a good crust underneath – otherwise they will stick.
→ If you cook your burgers on a barbecue, light the fire well in advance and make sure it has died down to glowing, reddish-grey coals before you start cooking.

John Torode's
Basic Beefburger

SERVES 6 LARGE BURGERS
→ 1.5KG (3¼LB) MINCED BEEF,
   IDEALLY CONTAINING
   40 PER CENT FAT
→ 2 RED ONIONS, FINELY DICED
→ A GOOD HANDFUL OF FLAT-LEAF
   PARSLEY, FINELY CHOPPED
→ 3 TBSP TOMATO KETCHUP
→ 3 TBSP OYSTER SAUCE
→ 1 EGG YOLK
   To serve:
→ 6 LARGE, SOFT WHITE BUNS,
   LIGHTLY TOASTED
→ LETTUCE, TOMATO, GHERKINS,
   ONION, AVOCADO, KETCHUP,
   MAYONNAISE – WHATEVER
   TAKES YOUR FANCY

1 Put all the ingredients in a large bowl. With your hands or a large spoon, mix everything together until it is evenly combined.

2 Divide the mixture into 6 portions and roll each one into a large ball. Flatten slightly with the palm of your hand, then place them in the fridge. If possible, chill for a good hour.

3 To cook the burgers, either have a barbecue good and hot, with the coals glowing, or heat a ridged griddle pan or heavy-based frying pan. Do not add any oil. Place the burgers on the barbecue rack or in the pan and leave for a few minutes, until the edges start to colour.

4 Slide a metal spatula under each burger and flip it over. Cook for a few minutes, then turn again. If using a frying pan or griddle pan, reduce the heat; on a barbecue just move the burgers to the sides, which should be slightly cooler. Leave the burgers to cook for anything from 8–15 minutes, depending on how well done you like them.

5 Serve in lightly toasted buns, with the accompaniments of your choice.

Inspired by contestant James Millen

Sirloin Steak with Black Pepper Crust and Rösti Potatoes

A great steak is something to be revered. Quality is paramount, so you should visit a good butcher's when shopping for this recipe. Treat the steak with the respect it deserves. To prevent it being overpowered by the pepper, sift the crushed peppercorns in a fine sieve to remove any dust before using. A generous garnish of watercress is needed to freshen up the dish.

- → 2 PARSNIPS, CHOPPED
- → 1 TBSP HORSERADISH SAUCE
- → 4 TABLESPOONS SINGLE CREAM
- → 50G (2OZ) BUTTER
- → 4 X 200G (7OZ) THICK SIRLOIN STEAKS
- → OIL FOR BRUSHING
- → 4 TBSP COARSELY CRUSHED BLACK PEPPERCORNS
- → 1 RAW BEETROOT, PARBOILED
- → 75G (3OZ) WATERCRESS
- → A FEW DROPS OF BALSAMIC VINEGAR
- → SALT AND FRESHLY GROUND BLACK PEPPER

For the rösti:
- → 550G (1¼LB) POTATOES, PREFERABLY KING EDWARD, PEELED AND GRATED
- → 1 ONION, FINELY CHOPPED
- → 25G (1OZ) LARDONS, FINELY CHOPPED
- → 1 EGG, BEATEN
- → 1 TBSP CHOPPED SAGE
- → 2 TSP GRAINY MUSTARD
- → 4 TBSP OLIVE OIL

MASTERCHEF TOP TIP
I know most people are concerned about the amount of fat they eat, and rightly so. But beef needs fat for flavour, so you must cook steak with a decent amount of fat still on. Just remember that you don't have to eat the fat; you can cut it off after cooking, if you want. Or put it to one side and I'll eat it!
Gregg Wallace, Masterchef Judge

1 For the rösti, put the grated potato in a sieve over a bowl. Season with plenty of salt to extract the juice and set aside for 20 minutes. Squeeze the potato dry between layers of kitchen paper.

2 Put the potato in a bowl with the onion, lardons, egg, sage and mustard and mix well. Shape the mixture into 8 flat cakes, either by hand or by pressing it into 7cm (2¾ in) metal rings.

3 Heat the olive oil in a large frying pan, add the rösti and fry until golden brown on each side. Drain on kitchen paper and keep warm.

4 Cook the parsnips in boiling salted water until tender, then drain well. Mash to a soft purée with the horseradish, cream and half the butter. Season to taste, then cover and keep warm.

5 Preheat a heavy-based frying pan or ridged griddle. Brush the steaks with oil and season with salt, then roll them in the black pepper.

6 Put the steaks in the pan and brown them quickly on both sides over a high heat, then reduce the heat and cook gently for the remaining time – about 4 minutes per side for a medium-rare steak. Leave to rest in a warm place.

7 Meanwhile, peel the beetroot and slice it thickly. Heat the remaining butter in a frying pan, add the beetroot slices and cook over a medium heat until crisp on the outside but tender inside.

8 Arrange the steaks, rösti, creamed parsnip and fried beetroot on serving plates. Garnish with the watercress and a few drops of balsamic vinegar. Serve immediately.

Masterchef Masterclass
John Torode's Steak

Cooking steak is deceptively simple. In theory, there's nothing more to it than slapping a steak in a hot pan. In practice, there are so many variables that you need to devote a little more care and attention to it than this might imply.

First, shop wisely for your steak. Visit a good butcher who will cut the steak to your liking and should be able to tell you something about the quality of the meat and where it came from. Alternatively, go direct to a producer – increasingly easy these days, with the spread of farmers' markets and Internet shopping (see List of Suppliers, pages 188–90).

Many people choose steak by looking for something that is uniformly red and not at all fatty, whereas a good steak needs some marbling – tiny veins of fat that melt into the meat and keep it moist during cooking. I prefer not to buy steak surrounded by yellow fat, as that usually means it comes from a herd that has been fed on grain rather than grass. Grass-fed herds, which will have been allowed to roam free, produce meat with milky-white fat that has the lovely, earthy flavour I prefer.

Fillet is usually thought of as the best cut, and because you get only two very small fillets from each beast, the laws of supply and demand dictate that it is extremely expensive. Sirloin is usually seen as next best, with rump coming a poor third. Ever game for a bit of controversy, I disagree with this. I really love a thick piece of rump cut from a piece of beef that has been hung on the bone for twenty-one days to mature. Pan-fry it very quickly in a really hot pan, then finish it off in the oven for 5–10 minutes until it is medium rare – fantastic stuff! A really classy piece of rump has all the right ratios of fat, muscle structure, fibre and flavour.

Everyone has their own opinion about how they like their steak done. If you follow the guidelines below, you should end up with your personal idea of steak heaven.

→ Use a heavy-based frying pan or a cast-iron griddle to cook the steak. These retain the heat well and ensure it is evenly distributed.

→ Brush the steak, rather than the pan, with oil and season it with salt and pepper just before cooking. Then get the pan almost smoking hot, lay the steak in it and sear it over a very high heat without disturbing it. When it has browned and slightly caramelised underneath, turn and cook the other side.

→ For large, medium-rare steaks allow about 3 minutes per side. Increase or decrease this by about a minute per side if you prefer medium or rare steak respectively.

→ Alternatively, you can sear the steak briefly on each side, then transfer it to a hot oven (about 200°C/400°F/Gas Mark 6) for 5–8 minutes, depending on how well done you like it.

→ Let the steak rest on a warm plate for a few minutes before serving. This allows the tissues to relax and become more tender.

→ Finally, since cooking times can only ever be approximate, it is worth knowing a chef's trick for testing whether steak is done to your liking. It works better for a firmer steak such as sirloin or rump rather than fillet, as fillet tends to be very spongy. While the steak is cooking, touch it with your finger. Then, using your right hand place the tip of your thumb on the tip of your little finger. Now touch the cushion of fat at the base of your thumb with your left hand – the resistance given by the thumb in this position is the same as a well-done steak. Open your right hand completely and relax it, then touch the cushion beneath your thumb again – the resistance felt now is the same as rare steak. Halfway between will be medium.

John Torode's
Steak Béarnaise

SERVES 4
→ 4 RUMP OR SIRLOIN STEAKS, WEIGHING ABOUT 300G (11OZ) EACH
→ A LITTLE OLIVE OIL
→ SALT AND FRESHLY GROUND BLACK PEPPER
→ A BUNCH OF WATERCRESS, TO SERVE
For the béarnaise sauce:
→ A FEW SPRIGS OF TARRAGON
→ 100ML (3½FL OZ) WHITE WINE VINEGAR
→ 1 SHALLOT, CHOPPED
→ 2 EGG YOLKS
→ 120G (4½OZ) WARM MELTED BUTTER

MASTERCHEF TOP TIP
As with mustard or horseradish sauce, béarnaise should be served in small quantities alongside the meat or fish but never over it.

Steak with béarnaise sauce is a classic dish that will never go out of fashion – especially when served with a bowl of crisp, freshly cooked chips (see page 66). Béarnaise is similar to hollandaise (see pages 20–1) but even richer, and flavoured with tarragon. Used as an accompaniment to meat and fish, it is always served at room temperature and should have a good kick to it from the initial vinegar reduction.

1 To make the sauce, strip the tarragon leaves from their stalks, chop them and set aside. Crush the stalks between your fingers to release the oils.

2 Put the vinegar, shallot and tarragon stalks in a small saucepan and bring to the boil. Simmer until reduced by about three-quarters, then leave to cool.

3 Strain the vinegar reduction into a heatproof glass bowl. Place the bowl over a pan of barely simmering water, making sure the water does not touch the base of the bowl.

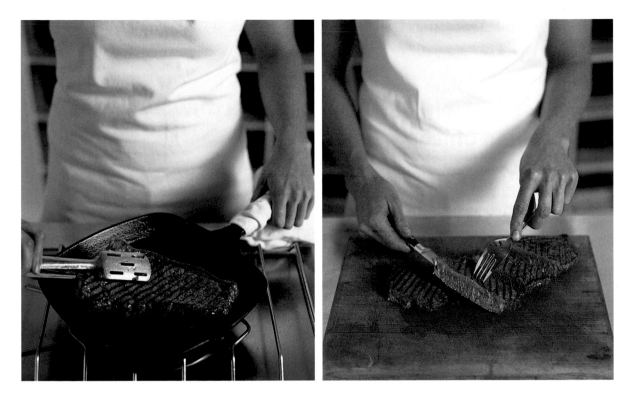

Add the egg yolks and whisk for 2–3 minutes, until the mixture turns pale and thick and the whisk leaves a trail on the surface when lifted.

4 Remove the bowl from the heat and put it on a folded cloth on a work surface. Start to whisk in the melted butter, little by little, making sure that each addition has been thoroughly incorporated before the next. Continue whisking in this way until all the butter has been used or your arm has fallen off! If the sauce gets too thick at any stage, add a few drops of hot water from the saucepan.

5 Season the sauce with salt and pepper and stir in the chopped tarragon. The sauce should taste sharp and well seasoned. Remember that it is for flavouring the meat and should have a good punch to it.

6 Preheat a heavy frying pan or a ridged griddle until almost smoking hot. Season the steaks with lots of salt and pepper and rub well with olive oil, then cook as described on page 107. Rest briefly in a warm place, then serve with the watercress and béarnaise sauce on the side.

Salads and Vegetarian

Masterchef Masterclass
John Torode's Vinaigrette and Mayonnaise

Salad dressings such as mayonnaise and vinaigrette can enhance the humble lettuce leaf and bring a new dimension to even the simplest salads. Mayonnaise is one of the most versatile sauces ever invented, yet it is based on just two ingredients: eggs and oil. To that base you can add a variety of flavourings: lemon, mustard or garlic; blanched green vegetables such as spinach and watercress; herbs such as basil, parsley, dill, tarragon and chives; or piquant ingredients such as capers, horseradish, anchovies and finely chopped gherkins. Flavoured mayonnaise can be served not just with salads but with fish, poultry, meat and vegetables.

Like hollandaise (see pages 20–1), mayonnaise is an emulsified sauce. The secret of success is to beat the oil into the yolks very slowly – just a drop at a time initially – until the mixture thickens.

Vinaigrette is a simple oil and vinegar emulsion, which, unlike mayonnaise, is not expected to remain stable. It couldn't be easier to make but the crucial thing is to get the balance of flavours right. It should be tart but rounded, viscous but not oily, and full-flavoured but not overpowering. Its character varies depending on the type of oil used, the type of vinegar (or you can substitute lemon juice), and whether it includes mustard, herbs and other flavourings.

Here are some tips for success when making mayonnaise:

→ Make sure all the ingredients are at room temperature before you start, then the mixture is less likely to separate.

→ Rather than olive oil, I prefer to use vegetable oil. Olive oil is too strong and can leave an unpleasant aftertaste. If you use a generous amount of vinegar and mustard, they provide all the flavour you need.

→ Place the bowl on a cloth before you start whisking, to stop it moving around.

→ Add the oil to the other ingredients a drop at a time to begin with, whisking like crazy (it helps to have someone else adding the oil while you whisk). Then after you have added about a third of the oil and the emulsion has been established, you can pour in the rest in a thin, steady stream.

→ If the mayonnaise looks as if it is starting to curdle, you may be able to bring it back together by whisking in a few drops of hot water. If the worst happens and it separates, you can usually save it by starting again with another egg yolk in a clean bowl and whisking the separated mixture into it a drop at a time.

→ If the finished mayonnaise is too thick, whisk in a little hot water or lemon juice.

→ I always use white pepper rather than black for seasoning mayonnaise, so that the specks don't make the sauce look dirty.

John Torode's
Vinaigrette

MAKES ABOUT 400ML (14FL OZ)
→ 1 TBSP DIJON MUSTARD
→ 5 TBSP RED WINE VINEGAR
→ 1 TSP WALNUT OIL
→ 300ML (½ PINT) EXTRA
   VIRGIN OLIVE OIL
→ SEA SALT AND FRESHLY
   GROUND BLACK PEPPER

This is my favourite dressing, which I learned to make when I first started working in a commercial kitchen. It's good with crisp salad leaves such as Cos or iceberg, and also with asparagus or cooled, slightly underdone green beans.

When you are buying salad leaves, look for decent-sized heads that are as fresh as possible, without browned or wilting edges. The outer layer should be discarded (give it to your pet rabbit, if you have one), as it will have been exposed to the air and therefore not as crisp as the inner leaves.

Wash salad leaves gently in cool water. The way I do this is to fill the sink with water and drop the leaves on top. Then I gently push them under the water and turn them over to clean them. The dirt should sink to the bottom while the leaves float and escape bruising. Lift the leaves gently from the water a handful at a time, and either shake them dry or use a salad spinner.

Never drown your salad leaves in dressing: you should toss them in just enough dressing to coat. Too much will make the leaves limp and unpleasant in texture.

1 Place the mustard and vinegar in a bowl and whisk until blended.

2 Gradually whisk in the walnut and olive oils in a thin, steady stream, then season with salt and pepper. Taste and adjust the seasoning with more mustard, vinegar, oil, salt or pepper as necessary.

3 The vinaigrette will keep in an airtight jar in the fridge for up to 1 month. Bring to room temperature before using and whisk briefly (or shake the jar) to combine the ingredients.

John Torode's
Mayonnaise

MAKES ABOUT 300ML (½ PINT)
→ 3 EGG YOLKS
→ 1 TBSP DIJON MUSTARD
→ 1 TBSP WHITE WINE VINEGAR
→ 250ML (8FL OZ) VEGETABLE OIL
→ A SQUEEZE OF LEMON JUICE
→ SALT AND WHITE PEPPER

1 Put the egg yolks in a small bowl with the mustard and vinegar. Whisk together until smooth and almost white.

2 Add the oil a drop at a time, whisking constantly. After adding about a third of the oil, the mixture should have thickened considerably. Add a few drops of hot water if it is too thick to whisk.

3 Pour in the rest of the oil in a thin, steady stream, still whisking, until you have a smooth, glossy mayonnaise that is thick enough to stand in peaks.

4 Adjust the seasoning with lemon juice, salt and pepper, plus more vinegar if necessary. The mayonnaise will keep in the fridge for 4 days.

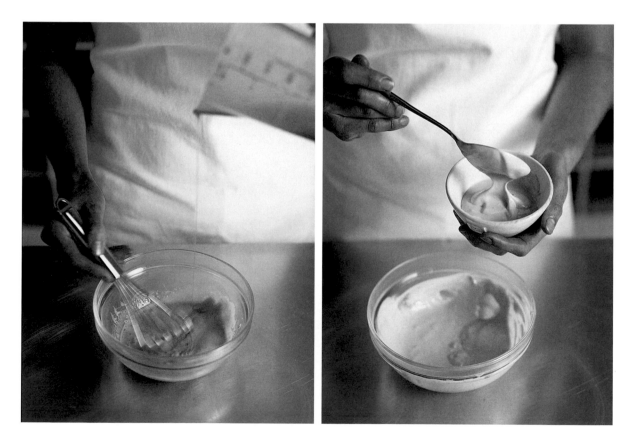

John Torode's
Aïoli

MAKES 350ML (12FL OZ)
- → 1 LARGE GARLIC CLOVE
- → 2 EGG YOLKS
- → 300ML (½ PINT) LIGHT OLIVE OIL
  (OR EQUAL PARTS EXTRA VIRGIN
  OLIVE OIL AND SUNFLOWER OIL)
- → JUICE OF ½ LEMON
- → SALT AND WHITE PEPPER

Aïoli is a garlic-flavoured mayonnaise originating from the South of France. It adds a real kick to hot dishes such as grilled fish and roast lamb, and also goes well with a plate of vegetable crudités for dipping. If the garlic clove has a green shoot down the centre, remove and discard it, as it can taste very bitter.

Aïoli doesn't keep well. Use it within a few hours of making, or the garlic flavour will become slightly rancid.

1 Peel, smash and finely chop the garlic, then place it in a bowl with the egg yolks.

2 Start to whisk in the oil drop by drop. As the mixture thickens and becomes stable, season with salt and white pepper, then whisk in a tablespoon of the lemon juice. Add a few drops of hot water if it becomes too thick.

3 Whisk in the remaining oil in a thin, steady stream, until you have a thick, glossy mixture. Taste and adjust the seasoning with more lemon juice, salt and pepper.

Inspired by contestant Milla Mackley

Pancetta and Dolcelatte Salad with Parsnip Crisps and Hazelnuts

This salad is a real find. The classic combination of spinach and blue cheese is given a lift by the addition of hazelnuts and parsnip. The dressing holds the salad together and gives it some zest.

→ 1 LARGE PARSNIP, PEELED
→ 100G (4OZ) PANCETTA, SLICED
→ 1 TBSP VEGETABLE OIL
→ 50G (2OZ) BLANCHED HAZELNUTS
→ 225G (8OZ) YOUNG LEAF SPINACH
→ 150G (5OZ) DOLCELATTE CHEESE, CUT INTO SMALL LUMPS
For the dressing:
→ 4 TBSP EXTRA VIRGIN OLIVE OIL
→ 1 SCANT TSP GOOD-QUALITY RED WINE VINEGAR (SUCH AS CABERNET SAUVIGNON)
→ SCANT 1/4 TSP DIJON MUSTARD
→ 1/2 GARLIC CLOVE, CRUSHED
→ A PINCH OF SUGAR
→ A PINCH EACH OF SALT AND PEPPER

1 Preheat the oven to 200ºC/400ºF/Gas Mark 6.

2 Slice the parsnip very thinly, preferably using a mandoline. Cook in boiling salted water for 30 seconds, then drain well and set aside.

3 Fry the pancetta in a non-stick frying pan until crisp, then drain well, reserving the fat. Stir the vegetable oil and the fat from the pancetta together and use to coat the parsnip slices lightly.

4 Spread the parsnip slices out on a baking tray lined with baking parchment. Place in the oven and cook for about 8 minutes, until crisp and golden brown. Remove from the oven and leave to cool.

5 Put the hazelnuts on a baking sheet and roast for about 5 minutes, until light golden. Remove from the oven and set aside.

6 Place the spinach leaves in a large serving bowl. Put all the ingredients for the dressing into a screw-top jar and shake vigorously to combine. Taste and adjust the seasoning if necessary. Drizzle a little of the dressing over the spinach and toss well, so the leaves are lightly coated.

7 Add the parsnip crisps, pancetta and dolcelatte cheese to the leaves and lightly toss together. Sprinkle the hazelnuts over the salad and serve immediately.

Warm Salad of Scallops, Black Pudding and Butternut Squash

Scallops and black pudding sound like an unlikely match but they work very well together. They do need some moisture to make them eat well, however. This recipe was cooked on the show without any dressing and it was a little dry. You could either make the dressing given below, or serve it with aïoli (see page 118).

Mashed potato with scallops and black pudding also works a treat, as does some very wet, piping-hot polenta.

→ 50G (2OZ) BUTTER
→ 1 BUTTERNUT SQUASH, PEELED, DESEEDED AND CUT INTO 5CM (2 IN) DICE
→ 2 TBSP LIGHT VEGETABLE OIL, PLUS A LITTLE EXTRA FOR BRUSHING
→ 1 BLACK PUDDING (ABOUT 250G/9OZ), CUT INTO SLICES 1CM (½ IN) THICK
→ 12 KING SCALLOPS
→ SALT AND FRESHLY GROUND BLACK PEPPER
→ LEMON SLICES AND SNIPPED CHIVES, TO GARNISH

For the dressing:
→ 4 TBSP EXTRA VIRGIN OLIVE OIL
→ 4 TBSP GROUNDNUT OIL
→ A PINCH OF SEA SALT
→ A PINCH OF WHITE PEPPER
→ 1 TBSP GOOD-QUALITY WHITE WINE VINEGAR
→ 2 TSP LEMON JUICE
→ 1 TBSP SNIPPED CHIVES

(m) MASTERCHEF TOP TIP
Buy good-quality scallops, preferably diver-caught ones, that have not been frozen and do not wash them – just wipe them clean with a dry cloth.
John Torode, Masterchef Judge

1 Put the butter, squash, 100ml (3½fl oz) water and some salt and pepper in a medium pan and bring to the boil. Simmer for 10 minutes or until the squash is tender, then strain off any excess liquid and reserve.

2 Mash the squash and adjust the seasoning. If the squash is dry, add a little of the reserved cooking liquid. Reheat gently, stirring constantly, until thick and smooth. Remove from the heat and keep warm.

3 Heat the oil in a frying pan and gently fry the black pudding in it until crisp. Remove from the pan and keep warm.

4 Lightly brush a ridged griddle pan or a heavy-based frying pan with a little oil and place it over a high heat until very hot. Season the scallops with a little salt, place them in the hot pan and sear for 1 minute on each side, until browned and lightly caramelised. Remove from the pan.

5 For the dressing, put all the ingredients in a bowl and whisk together until emulsified.

6 Place a good spoonful of the squash purée on 4 serving plates. Arrange the scallops and black pudding slices in overlapping layers on each plate and garnish with lemon slices. Drizzle the dressing over the warm scallop salad and serve immediately, sprinkled with snipped chives. (Any leftover dressing can be stored in the fridge for 2–3 days.)

Minted Prawn Salad

The combination of mint, parsley and coriander is not a new one. The Vietnamese have long used it to add freshness to salads and soups, which often contain sour flavours. Don't overcook the prawns, and serve this salad as soon as it is ready, otherwise it will go soggy and be unpleasant to eat.

→ 1 SMALL PARSNIP, SLICED ABOUT 2MM (1/12 IN) THICK
→ 4 TBSP VEGETABLE OIL
→ 550G (1¼LB) LARGE, HEADLESS RAW PRAWNS, SHELL ON
→ 200G (7OZ) BABY SALAD LEAVES
→ A HANDFUL OF FRESH CORIANDER, CHOPPED
→ 2 SPRIGS OF MINT, CHOPPED
→ A SPRIG OF FLAT-LEAF PARSLEY, CHOPPED
→ SALT AND FRESHLY GROUND BLACK PEPPER

For the dressing:
→ 1 SMALL, MILD RED CHILLI, FINELY CHOPPED
→ GRATED ZEST OF 1 LIME
→ 1 TABLESPOON LIME JUICE
→ 2 TBSP SOFT LIGHT BROWN SUGAR
→ 2 TBSP THAI FISH SAUCE (*NAM PLA*)
→ 4 TABLESPOONS LIGHT VEGETABLE OIL
→ A FEW DROPS OF SESAME OIL

1 Preheat the oven to 200°C/400°F/Gas Mark 6.

2 Cook the parsnip slices in boiling salted water until tender, then drain well and dry on kitchen paper. Spread out on a baking sheet and brush with a little of the vegetable oil. Bake for about 15 minutes, until crisp, then set aside.

3 Meanwhile, prepare the prawns by peeling off the shells, leaving the last tail segment in place. If the intestinal tract that runs down the back of each prawn is visible, remove it with the point of a sharp knife. Season the prawns and toss them in the remaining oil, then set aside.

4 For the dressing, place the chopped chilli in a bowl with the lime zest and juice. Whisk in the sugar, fish sauce, vegetable oil and sesame oil.

5 Heat a large, heavy-based frying pan over a high heat, tip the prawns into the pan and sear for 2 minutes on each side. Do not be tempted to shake the pan as they cook. When they are pink and cooked through, remove them from the pan and mix with the parsnip crisps. Fold in a little of the dressing.

6 Put the salad leaves on 4 serving plates and top with the prawn mixture. Mix the fresh herbs together and sprinkle them on top. Drizzle more dressing over the salad and serve immediately.

'I like the punch of the prawns and the dressing.'
John Torode, Masterchef Judge

Inspired by contestant Mark Rigby

Carpaccio with Rocket

Beef carpaccio – what a beauty! This was first served at Harry's Bar in Venice, and was named after the Renaissance Venetian painter. If you are not used to it, you may find the texture of raw beef a little strange but I love it. A good Caesar-style dressing also works well here. Serve with warm bread.

→ 400G (14OZ) BEST-QUALITY BEEF FILLET, WELL TRIMMED OF ANY FAT
→ JUICE OF ½ LEMON
→ 4 TBSP EXTRA VIRGIN OLIVE OIL
→ A LARGE HANDFUL OF ROCKET LEAVES
→ A SMALL BLOCK OF PARMESAN CHEESE
→ SALT AND FRESHLY GROUND BLACK PEPPER

MASTERCHEF TOP TIP
Carpaccio must be made with beef fillet that has been well hung to mature it. Before cutting the meat, roll it very tightly in cling film, then chill it as much as possible without actually freezing it. This will give a good round shape and will make cutting thin slices much easier. As an alternative way of serving it, you could briefly deep-fry the rocket, sprinkle with toasted sesame seeds and extra virgin olive oil, and serve with hot olive, sage and onion bread.
Peter Richards, Masterchef Mentor

1 Using a very sharp knife, cut the beef into paper-thin slices. Lay the slices between 2 sheets of greaseproof paper and flatten with a meat mallet or a rolling pin – the thinner the better.

2 Whisk the lemon juice and oil together to make a dressing.

3 Lightly season the rocket with salt and pepper. Scatter the rocket over a serving platter and arrange the beef slices on top.

4 Brush the beef with the dressing. Using a potato peeler, shave the Parmesan over the beef slices. Serve with warm bread.

'I want to get through to the next stage . . . I want to get to the end . . . I want to win it!'
Mark Rigby, Contestant

Masterchef Masterclass
John Torode's Egg Basics

In the UK we consume nearly 30 million eggs a day, yet for something so fundamental to our diet we seem to know very little about how to cook them. Isn't it time we stopped taking eggs for granted and began to appreciate them more? Beautifully encased in their pristine shells, eggs are the perfect nutritional package: an excellent source of protein, vitamins and iron. In culinary terms, their uses are astonishingly varied: they can be boiled, baked, fried, scrambled, poached or made into omelettes. They form the basis of soufflés, custards, batters, meringues, and sauces such as hollandaise and mayonnaise. And they have an important role in enriching, thickening and binding sweet and savoury dishes.

Few of us nowadays are privileged enough to have a few hens out the back but we can still try to buy eggs that are as fresh as possible. Buy organic if you can – the birds will have been kept fairly and not subjected to undue stress. Furthermore, they will have been fed a good diet that doesn't include routine antibiotics. The colour of the shell has no effect on the flavour of the egg, it is simply a result of the breed of hen.

You can test how fresh an egg is by placing it in a bowl of water: if the egg lays flat, it is fresh; if it starts to stand up, or even floats, it is time for it to go in the bin.

Another way of testing for freshness is to break an egg on to a plate: the white should be jelly-like and hold the yolk up in a well-formed mound. If the white is watery and the yolk flat, the egg is old – still usable but best for baking.

All eggs that are to be eaten hot should be served as soon as they are ready. The white and yolk are made primarily of protein, which changes in colour and form when you apply heat to it. In the case of a boiled egg in particular, it will continue to cook when taken from the heat. This is why you sometimes end up with a hard-boiled egg when you are convinced it should be soft.

John Torode's
Basic Boiled Egg

Eggs that are a few days old are best for boiling. As the egg ages, natural gases accumulate between the shell and the fine membrane holding the white. A fresh egg will be harder to peel. The timings given below are for medium eggs.

Boiled eggs to be served hot

Place the eggs in a pan with plenty of room for them to move around. Fill with cold water and place over a high heat. Bring just to the boil, then reduce to a simmer (this will stop the eggs bashing into each other). Once simmering, for soft-boiled eggs, cook for 3 minutes, then remove from the heat and serve immediately, with toast soldiers, a large knob of butter, and some salt and pepper. For hard-boiled eggs, cook for $4\frac{1}{2}$–5 minutes.

Boiled eggs to be served cold

For the perfect soft-boiled salad egg, bring a pan of water to the boil, gently lower in the eggs and return to the boil. Reduce the heat to a simmer and cook for exactly $4\frac{1}{2}$ minutes. Lift the eggs from the water, place in a bowl of cold water and run water from the tap over the top until they are cool. Keep them immersed in the water when peeling, to prevent them breaking up, and store them in fresh water if you are not using them straight away. For hard-boiled eggs, increase the cooking time to $5\frac{1}{2}$ minutes.

Name: Rachel Szadura
Age: 39
Occupation: Trying 24-7 to get on television, cooking!
Place of residence: Bakewell, Derbyshire
Why did you apply to Masterchef?
Because I felt that as a true foodie and someone who's extremely passionate, I thought I had what it takes to win the competition.
What do you cook at home and who do you cook for?
I'm constantly entertaining – we have friends round all the time. I mostly cook English, Italian and Indian food. I have a large circle of friends and they often take 40- or 50-mile detours to come to my house because they know I'll always be knocking something up in the kitchen. Believe you me, I'm the real domestic goddess.
What is your favourite meal?
I couldn't possibly say; I have too many favourites!
What are your aspirations in the world of cooking and food?
I want to be on television cooking and be known to the whole nation as 'the Kitten in the Kitchen'! I would also love to meet Gordon Ramsay – he would meet his match. And I'd love to be the face of a major food retailer – just like Jamie Oliver!

Name: Scott Ball
Age: 32
Occupation: Computer and business consultant.
Place of residence: East London
Why did you apply to Masterchef?
I really love food – I'm not a petite flower! I've always had a passion for food and a passion for cooking and I thought it would be a great avenue for furthering my cooking skills.
What do you cook at home and who do you cook for?
I cook for my partner and friends and I cook everything! I'm a bit of a crazy chef, I'm inspired by ingredients. I'm also a keen gardener, so I grow a lot of my own fruit and vegetables on my allotment and I have a passion for the whole cycle from growing to cooking. I particularly love modern comfort foods; most are simple yet decadent at the same time.
What is your favourite meal?
Sausage and mash, because it's good, hardy, filling, simplistic food. If you have great sausages, they make a fantastic meal.
What are your aspirations in the world of cooking and food?
Some day I would really like to either open a restaurant or a gourmet food shop, getting the food and delivering the right ingredients to people.

Name: Thomasina Miers
Age: 28
Occupation: I'm currently compiling a cookbook that will be published next September.
Place of residence: West London
Why did you apply to Masterchef?
I was in Ireland, staying on a cheese farm I used to work at, looking at some magazines, and saw an article on the series and filled in the application form for fun. I never dreamed that anyone would call me up.
What do you cook at home and who do you cook for?
I cook for my friends all the time, and I cook pretty much everything. I live near some great Middle Eastern produce shops, so I cook a lot of food from that region. I live with an Italian chef, so we cook a lot of Italian too. I also cook Mexican food – I worked in Mexico helping some people to set up a restaurant and bar, and toured around Mexico for two months. I love experimenting with new flavours.
What is your favourite meal?
I love eating everything! I love Spanish food and I love chorizo with anything.
What are your aspirations in the world of cooking and food?
I guess it would always be to learn more and inspire other people with what I've learned. There's so much I want to do.

Gougère with Mushrooms in Marsala Sauce

As with asparagus in May, when wild mushrooms come into season in autumn, we get such a limited time to eat them that it's tempting to gorge ourselves!

→ 25G (1OZ) BUTTER
→ 2 SHALLOTS, FINELY CHOPPED
→ 1 GARLIC CLOVE, FINELY CHOPPED
→ 400G (14OZ) MUSHROOMS (A MIXTURE OF WILD AND CHESTNUT MUSHROOMS), SLICED
→ 1 TBSP CHOPPED FLAT-LEAF PARSLEY
→ SALT AND FRESHLY GROUND BLACK PEPPER

For the choux pastry:
→ 100G (4OZ) PLAIN FLOUR
→ A PINCH OF SALT
→ A PINCH OF CAYENNE PEPPER
→ 75G (3OZ) BUTTER, DICED
→ 3 EGGS, BEATEN
→ 25G (1OZ) GRUYÈRE CHEESE, GRATED
→ 25G (1OZ) PARMESAN CHEESE, FINELY GRATED

For the marsala sauce:
→ 15G (½OZ) BUTTER
→ 1 LARGE SHALLOT, FINELY CHOPPED
→ 100ML (3½FL OZ) DRY MARSALA
→ 250ML (8FL OZ) DOUBLE CREAM

For the watercress salad:
→ 100G (4OZ) WATERCRESS
→ 2–3 TSP OLIVE OIL
→ 1 TSP LEMON JUICE

1 Preheat the oven to 200°C/400°F/Gas Mark 6.

2 To make the choux pastry, sift the flour, salt and cayenne pepper into a bowl and set aside. Put the butter and 215 ml (7½ fl oz) water in a small, heavy-based saucepan. Heat gently, then bring to a full boil. Remove from the heat and immediately drop in all the seasoned flour. Whisk vigorously until the mixture leaves the side of the pan. Cool slightly, then whisk in the beaten egg a little at a time, using a hand-held electric beater and whisking well after each addition. You may not need all the egg; the mixture should have a fairly firm dropping consistency. Carry on beating until the paste has a definite sheen, then beat in the cheese.

3 Grease 2 large baking trays. Pile 2 high mounds of the mixture on to each tray to make 4 large buns, leaving room for them to spread. Bake in 2 batches for 30 minutes. Do not open the oven door during the cooking time or they will collapse.

4 Remove the buns from the oven when they are dark golden and crisp. Cut off a lid from each bun and set aside. Scrape out any wet paste with a teaspoon and discard. Keep the buns warm.

5 For the marsala sauce, melt the butter in a small frying pan, add the shallot and fry over a medium heat until soft and translucent. Pour in the marsala and simmer until reduced by half. Stir in the cream and simmer until reduced by half again. Season to taste, then remove from the heat, cover and keep warm.

6 To make the filling, melt the butter in a large frying pan, add the shallots and garlic and fry until soft and translucent. Add the mushrooms and sauté until tender. Pour the marsala sauce over the mushroom mixture and stir lightly to combine. Gently stir in the parsley, then taste and adjust the seasoning.

7 Place the choux buns on 4 plates, pile the mushroom mixture into them and top with the reserved lids. Toss the watercress with the olive oil and lemon juice, season, and serve with the buns.

Masterchef Masterclass
John Torode's Omelette

Almost everybody makes omelettes but unfortunately very few people make them well. They should be cooked slowly in a generous amount of butter and seasoned well with white pepper rather than black. They should be soft and slightly runny – or baveuse, as the French call it – and have very little colour on the outside. They should look thick and sumptuous, like a soft pillow. And they should be served hot. Most of the time, omelettes are served in completely the opposite fashion, as horrid, hard, overcooked slabs of egg.

Flat omelettes, such as the Spanish tortilla and the Italian frittata, are a different thing altogether from the classic omelette – and, though I admit I'm partisan, as far away from a beautiful, soft omelette as a Robin Reliant is from a classic sports car.

A good omelette takes practice but it is worth it. Keep it simple, follow the tips below, and don't start experimenting with fillings until you have mastered the basic plain version.

→ The correct pan is vital for cooking omelettes. It should be made of cast iron, preferably with a non-stick surface, and should have sloping sides so you can slide the omelette out easily. For a 3-egg omelette you will need an 18cm (7 in) pan.

→ Use really good, fresh eggs and butter, so the omelette is well flavoured rather than bland.

→ Beat the eggs thoroughly before cooking, to give an even, homogeneous mixture.

→ Be sure to cook the omelette at the correct heat level: too high and it will be tough and dry; too low and it will be flat and more like scrambled egg. The entire cooking time shouldn't be more than 3–4 minutes.

→ Remember that the omelette will continue to cook in its own heat after you take it off the hob, so make sure the mixture is still slightly runny in the centre.

→ Always serve omelettes straight away, on a hot plate, so they don't cool down and become tough.

John Torode's
Basic Omelette

SERVES 1
→ 3 LARGE EGGS
→ 2 TEASPOONS DOUBLE CREAM
  (OPTIONAL)
→ 50G (2OZ) BUTTER
→ SALT AND WHITE PEPPER

1 Break the eggs into a mixing bowl and add the cream, if using. Mix well with a fork, then season with salt and pepper.

2 Place an omelette pan over a medium heat and add the butter. When it is melted and starting to foam, reduce the heat and pour in the egg. Gently move it around with a fork for a few seconds so it starts to cook evenly.

3 Using the fork, draw back the set egg around the edges and tilt the pan, so the uncooked egg flows out to the sides. Cook for a few seconds longer, until the underneath is lightly coloured but the top still moist.

4 Raise the pan, as if you were showing someone the contents, but leave the far end resting on the hob. Using a spatula or a fork, ease the raised end of the omelette over so it starts to roll. Fold the omelette over and tip it on to a warm plate. Serve immediately.

Fillings

Fillings that don't need cooking, such as chopped herbs or grated cheese, can be added just before you fold the omelette; the cheese will start to melt in the heat of the eggs. Fillings such as mushrooms or bacon should be cooked in a separate pan, then added to the omelette before folding.

Posh Mushrooms on Toast

This dish makes a wonderful starter. It calls for a good-sized glass of robust red wine to go with it. At the beginning of autumn, wild mushrooms are readily available and many are from the UK.

→ 1 TBSP OLIVE OIL
→ 50G (2OZ) SMOKED PANCETTA, DICED
→ 1–2 GARLIC CLOVES, FINELY CHOPPED
→ 25G (1OZ) UNSALTED BUTTER
→ 200G (7OZ) MIXED WILD MUSHROOMS (SUCH AS CHANTERELLES, CEPS AND MORELS), CUT IN HALF IF LARGE
→ 3 TBSP DRY WHITE WINE
→ 3 TBSP ROUGHLY CHOPPED FLAT-LEAF PARSLEY
→ 4 SLICES OF SOURDOUGH BREAD OR SIMILAR
→ SALT AND FRESHLY GROUND BLACK PEPPER

1 Heat the oil in a large frying pan, add the pancetta and fry until golden brown, stirring occasionally. Add the garlic and cook over a low heat until soft and translucent.

2 Raise the heat a little and add a small knob of the butter. When it starts to foam, stir in the mushrooms and cook for 2–3 minutes.

3 Add the wine and let it bubble until almost evaporated. Season with plenty of salt and pepper, stir in the parsley and set aside.

4 Toast the bread on a ridged griddle pan or under the grill. Use the remaining butter to spread on the toast. Top with the mushroom mixture and serve immediately.

MASTERCHEF TOP TIP

If you ever go foraging for mushrooms, never, and I mean NEVER, eat anything you don't recognise. Some fungi are extremely poisonous. On the other hand, buying wild mushrooms from food shops is as safe as a very safe thing on National Safe Day! Some packs of wild mushrooms contain cultivated 'wild' varieties – oyster and shiitake, for example. I don't know about you, but I don't think wild means farmed! To clean mushrooms, gently remove the dirt with a soft brush. Don't wash them, or they will get waterlogged and become slimy when cooked.
Gregg Wallace, Masterchef Judge

'John, you're a judge, not the Spanish Inquisition!'
Gregg Wallace, Masterchef Judge

Masterchef Masterclass
John Torode's Tomato Sauce

The simplest and best sauce for pasta is a well-seasoned, beautifully cooked tomato sauce. The most successful way to make it is not with fresh tomatoes but with canned ones, which will have been picked when ripe and preserved in a good amount of their own juice.

Tomatoes first appeared in Italy in the late sixteenth century but it wasn't until the eighteenth century that they became widely used in cooking. In the early nineteenth century, an enterprising Neapolitan company started canning local tomatoes for export, and this is still the best way to taste a true Italian tomato outside Italy. Top-quality canned tomatoes are sweet, with a good flesh-to-seed ratio, and keep their deep-red colour even after being subjected to the high heat used by the canning industry. Most of the fresh tomatoes on offer in supermarkets have been selected for their looks rather than their taste. They are quick-growing varieties, developed to have thick skins so they have a long shelf life and don't bruise easily. Tomatoes labelled 'vine-ripened' tend to be superior but you pay a premium for them.

I have one little thing to whinge about. I don't understand why people dismember a fresh tomato in the name of culinary art. They blanch them, skin them, cut them into quarters, remove the seeds and then cut the sodden flesh into little squares. Do they really think little squares of boiled tomato taste nice?

It's cheaper, quicker and more convenient to use canned tomatoes for pasta sauces. It will also give a much better result, especially if you follow the tips below:

→ Buy good-quality Italian canned tomatoes, as some cheaper brands contain a lot of water.
→ Don't boil the sauce rapidly, or it will evaporate too quickly and become bitter and solid.
→ Cooking gently is the key, and stirring well so the sauce does not stick to the bottom of the pan.
→ Mix the sauce thoroughly with hot pasta immediately before serving. It should be shiny from the olive oil and not sticky at all.

John Torode's
Basic Tomato Sauce

MAKES ENOUGH FOR 500G (1LB 2OZ) PASTA

→ 4 TBSP OLIVE OIL
→ 1 ONION, DICED
→ 1 GARLIC CLOVE, CRUSHED
→ 1 TSP SEA SALT
→ 1 TSP FRESHLY GROUND BLACK PEPPER
→ 2 X 400G (14OZ) CANS OF CHOPPED TOMATOES
→ CHOPPED BASIL AND FRESHLY GRATED PARMESAN CHEESE, TO SERVE

1 Heat the oil in a heavy-based pan over a moderate heat. Add the onion and cook, stirring constantly, for 3 minutes, until softened. Add the garlic, salt and pepper and cook for 2 minutes.

2 Add the tomatoes and bring to the boil. Reduce the heat to a simmer and cook for 6–8 minutes, stirring occasionally, until the sauce is slightly thickened.

3 Take off the heat and toss with freshly cooked pasta. Serve sprinkled with chopped fresh basil and Parmesan cheese.

4 If you don't want to use the sauce straight away, it will keep, covered, in the fridge for a week, or in the freezer for about 3 months. You can also adapt it to use on pizzas by cooking it for about 10 minutes longer, until it has thickened and most of the juices have evaporated.

Inspired by contestant Shel Musiker

Goat's Cheese and Red Onion Tarts

Goat's cheese and red onions always work a treat together. The great thing about these tarts is that they fit into any season – try taking them on a picnic in the summer sun, or eat them hot for a winter supper. They also make a wonderful vegetarian dish.

→ 375G (13OZ) PUFF PASTRY
→ 50G (2OZ) BUTTER
→ 2 LARGE RED ONIONS, THINLY SLICED
→ A FEW SPRIGS OF THYME
→ 1 TSP WHITE WINE VINEGAR
→ 175G (6OZ) GOAT'S CHEESE LOG,
  CUT INTO THIN SLICES
→ 1 SMALL EGG, LIGHTLY BEATEN
→ SALT AND FRESHLY
  GROUND BLACK PEPPER

1 Preheat the oven to 220°C/425°F/Gas Mark 7.

2 Roll the pastry out to about 5mm (¼ in) thick. Cut out four 15cm (6 in) rounds, using a small plate as a guide. Place the rounds of pastry on a lightly greased baking sheet. Using a sharp knife, mark a 1cm (½ in) rim around the edge of the pastry, making sure you don't cut right through it. Lightly prick the area inside the rim with a fork. Chill for 30 minutes.

3 Melt the butter in a heavy-based frying pan over a medium heat. Add the onions and thyme and cook, stirring frequently, for 4–5 minutes. Add the vinegar, reduce the heat and cook until the onions are soft. Remove from the heat, discard the thyme and leave to cool.

4 Divide the onion mixture between the pastry bases, leaving the rim free. Top with the goat's cheese slices and season with salt and pepper.

5 Lightly brush the rim of the pastry with beaten egg. Bake for 15–20 minutes, until the pastry is well risen and golden brown. Remove from the oven and serve immediately.

Masterchef Masterclass
John Torode's Risotto

There is something wonderfully comforting about a risotto. It is warming, creamy and filling, and when cooked well it is one of the most delicious dishes in the world. The classic risottos are the best, as the simpler the flavours the more intense the end product.

To make a great risotto, you need patience and time. Not a great deal of time, though – say, 40 minutes in total, with 20 minutes of that going on the preparation and 20 minutes on the cooking. You also need to devote your attention to it fully while it cooks, stirring it almost constantly and maintaining a consistent heat level. You will be rewarded with that unique creamy texture, with each grain of rice tender yet still slightly firm in the centre.

Risotto is made with just a handful of ingredients but they must be of good quality. The rice in particular is paramount. Italian short grain rice, grown in the north of the country, is uniquely suited to risotto. It can absorb a great deal of liquid during cooking without breaking up, and it is high in starch, which dissolves into the liquid and thickens it. Arborio is the best-known variety, while the slightly more expensive carnaroli and vialone nano are becoming increasingly available in this country.

'Did you know that you should only ever stir risotto in one direction? . . . All the grains roll together and in doing so they never break up.'
John Torode, Masterchef Judge

No matter how you flavour a risotto, the basic technique is the same every time. Here are the essential steps for success:

→ Choose a heavy-based pan that is large enough to allow the rice to swell by about three times its volume.

→ The flavour base of most risottos consists of finely chopped shallot sweated in butter and/or oil. Keep the heat low at this stage, so the shallot becomes soft and translucent but does not colour. Then add the rice and stir it around for a few minutes until it is coated in the fat; this will prevent it sticking.

→ Keep the stock at simmering point in a separate pan so the temperature of the rice doesn't drop when you add it. Otherwise, the rice may be cooked on the outside before it is ready on the inside.

→ Add the stock a ladleful at a time, stirring constantly and letting it be absorbed by the rice before you add more. Be careful not to beat the mixture. Just stir it gently and carefully, scraping it up from the base of the pan, so the rice absorbs the liquid evenly. Do this over a moderate heat; the rice should be ticking over at a gentle simmer. If the heat is too high, the rice will move around too much and break up; if it is too low, the rice will become glutinous and heavy.

→ The cooking time from the moment you add the rice should be 15–20 minutes. When the risotto is done, it should be neither stiff nor runny, with the rice lightly bound together yet the grains still separate.

→ The classic way to finish a risotto is by vigorously beating butter and Parmesan into it to enrich it. This is known as the *mantecatura*.

→ Finally, always serve risotto straight away. It becomes stodgy if it is kept waiting.

'It's comfort food, it's wonderful food . . . and the good thing about a risotto is that it will absorb so many other flavours.'
Gregg Wallace, Masterchef Judge

Desserts

Baked Honey Peaches with Spiced Yoghurt

This simple treatment really brings out the best in peaches. The rich and perfumed flavour of the stone fruit, with its concentrated sweetness, is complemented by the spiced yoghurt. Nectarines would work equally well.

→ 4 RIPE PEACHES, HALVED AND STONED
→ 50G (2OZ) FLAKED ALMONDS
→ 4 TBSP ORANGE BLOSSOM HONEY
→ 4 TBSP CASTER SUGAR
→ A TINY PINCH OF SAFFRON (4–5 STRANDS)
→ GRATED ZEST AND JUICE OF 1 ORANGE
→ 2 TBSP BRANDY
→ ½ TSP GROUND CINNAMON
→ 150G (5OZ) GREEK-STYLE YOGHURT

1 Preheat the oven to 180°C/350°F/Gas Mark 4.

2 Arrange the peaches cut-side up in an ovenproof dish. Mix the almonds and honey together and place in the cavity of the peach halves. Sprinkle half the sugar on top.

3 Dry-roast the saffron for a few seconds in a small saucepan over a low heat, then stir in the rest of the sugar plus the orange zest and juice. Remove from the heat and leave to infuse for 10 minutes. Stir in the brandy and pour around the peaches.

4 Place in the oven and bake for 20 minutes, until the peaches are tender. Place 2 peach halves on each serving plate and spoon some of the fruit liquor on top. Mix the cinnamon into the yoghurt and serve with the fruit.

'Looking for new ideas, new ingredients, being creative and not producing poncey food! That's what's important.'
Peter Richards, Masterchef Mentor

Name: Helen Cristofoli
Age: 39
Occupation: I have my own food and drink PR business.
Place of residence: London
Why did you apply to Masterchef?
Because I fancied a new challenge in my life. I love food and I wanted to see how far I could get. Also because I had no idea how scary it would be!
What do you cook at home and who do you cook for?
I live alone, but I cook for friends and family and have lots of dinner parties. I cook everything from Italian and Chinese to Thai and more. I'm very adventurous. I'll try everything. Instead of Turkey for Christmas last year I devised lots of dishes all based around fish; then I cooked home-made spring rolls, duck with pancakes, lemon chicken, and loads of different recipes from scratch for Chinese New Year too. And for my therapy, I bake cakes when I want to relax.
What is your favourite meal?
Chocolate, chocolate and more chocolate! But if I had to make a meal it would be a risotto, because it's Italian and I'm Italian. It's cosy and homely.
What are your aspirations in the world of cooking and food?
The Masterchef experience gave me the confidence to leave the job I was doing and set up by myself. As long as I'm happy doing what I'm doing with food and drink and learning, I am happy, but I would love to eventually present or write about food and drink. And invent a low-calorie chocolate cake!

Name: James Cross
Age: 24
Occupation: I'm an organic vegetable farmer, but I'm also a year away from qualifying as a barrister.
Place of residence: Birmingham
Why did you apply to Masterchef?
It was chance really. I was talking to a member of my family, they'd seen the form in a magazine and I filled it out not really expecting anything to come of it. I never really had a desire to be a TV cook. I was very excited to get a phone call from a researcher and then started to take it all more seriously.
What do you cook at home and who do you cook for?
I cook for my girlfriend, friends and family. I cook anything that's seasonal. Seasonality is my thing – I'd rather do without asparagus in November and wait until it's ready to pick from the ground in April.
What is your favourite meal?
My favourite time of year for eating is mid-autumn. I love it when wild mushrooms come out. I pick them and sell chanterelles and trompettes to restaurants and cook with them at home. I've picked 17 of the top variety for eating, and that's on the outskirts of Birmingham! I'd love to find a truffle.
What are your aspirations in the world of cooking and food?
My aspiration in the world of cooking is to eat well. My long-term goal would be to supply really good-quality ingredients and delicacies from around the world to the best restaurants.

Name: Simon Cathcart
Age: 34
Occupation: I work as a purchasing consultant to the hospitality industry.
Place of residence: South of Glasgow
Why did you apply to Masterchef?
I saw the advert online and sent in an application straight away. I knew it was something I wanted to do. I love cooking, going on national TV appealed to me and I'm a real foodie!
What do you cook at home and who do you cook for?
I do all of the cooking at home – for dinner parties, for my wife and my kids. I love to get the kids involved in cooking, to try things they haven't had before, to learn what's good and bad for you. I find cooking really therapeutic, so quite often I just cook for myself. You don't have to be overly fancy for things to taste good, but I do spend a long time making sure things are well presented. I aspire to Michelin star level!
What is your favourite meal?
I love cooking with fish and seafood especially. There is so much variety in the textures and flavours in seafood and there are so many ways of cooking it.
What are your aspirations in the world of cooking and food?
Ultimately I want to own my own restaurant. I've always had a hankering to have my own restaurant ever since I was the only boy in my Home Economics class at school. I want to use my own ideas, innovation and cooking skills.

Ginger Upside-down Cakes with Ginger Crème Fraîche and Caramelised Figs

These little puddings are quintessential comfort food. A good helping of custard would not be out of place. The ginger syrup is one of those useful baking ingredients that can change an otherwise plain pudding into something both flavourful and moist, as it helps to stabilise the mixture.

→ 75G (3OZ) UNSALTED BUTTER, PLUS A SMALL KNOB OF BUTTER FOR GREASING
→ 75G (3OZ) CASTER SUGAR, PLUS A LITTLE EXTRA FOR DUSTING
→ 3–4 PIECES OF STEM GINGER IN SYRUP, SLICED INTO THIN ROUNDS
→ 4 TSP SYRUP FROM THE STEM GINGER JAR
→ 1 EGG, LIGHTLY BEATEN
→ GRATED ZEST OF 1 LEMON
→ 75G (3OZ) SELF-RAISING FLOUR

For the caramelised figs:
→ 4 FRESH FIGS, QUARTERED
→ 200G (7OZ) CASTER SUGAR

For the ginger crème fraîche:
→ 200G (7OZ) CRÈME FRAÎCHE
→ 3 TBSP SYRUP FROM THE STEM GINGER JAR

MASTERCHEF TOP TIP
When you are buying figs, to find really ripe ones pick them up gently and look underneath. If there are little droplets that look like leaking sap, take them home and eat them immediately – they're beautifully ripe!
John Torode, Masterchef Judge

1 Preheat the oven to 180°C/350°F/Gas Mark 4.

2 Grease 4 ramekin dishes with the knob of butter and dust them with a little caster sugar. Line the base of each dish with the ginger slices and spoon a teaspoon of the ginger syrup on top.

3 Cream the butter and caster sugar together until light and fluffy. Gradually add the egg, beating well after each addition, then stir in the lemon zest. Sift in the flour and gently fold it in, using a large metal spoon. Divide the mixture between the ramekins and level the surface. Put the ramekins in a roasting tin containing enough hot water to come halfway up the sides of the dishes. Bake for 30 minutes, until risen and golden.

4 Meanwhile, put the quartered figs on to a baking tray lined with baking parchment. Gently heat the caster sugar in a medium heavy-based saucepan until it melts. Raise the heat and cook, without stirring, until it turns a light golden brown. Immediately pour this caramel over the fig quarters and leave to cool.

5 When the puddings are done, remove them from the oven and leave to cool for a few minutes, then turn them out on to individual plates.

6 Mix the crème fraîche and stem ginger syrup in a bowl. Place the caramelised figs and 2 tablespoons of ginger crème fraîche on each plate with the ginger upside-down cake. Serve warm.

'I adored that pud – I could have eaten a bucketful!'
Gregg Wallace, Masterchef Judge

Inspired by contestant Katherine Haworth

Mango and Ginger Flapjack Crumble

Katherine continued to thrill all through her journey. This flapjack crumble makes a perfect family dessert, with just the right combination of crisp topping and soft fruit.

→ 1 RIPE MANGO, PEELED, STONED
  AND FINELY DICED
→ 1 PIECE OF STEM GINGER IN SYRUP,
  FINELY CHOPPED
→ 25G (1OZ) BUTTER
→ 1 TBSP DEMERARA SUGAR
→ 2 TBSP GOLDEN SYRUP
→ 75G (3OZ) PORRIDGE OATS
→ ½ TSP GROUND GINGER
→ 4 TBSP GREEK YOGHURT

1 Preheat the oven to 160°C/325°F/Gas Mark 3.

2 Mix the mango and stem ginger together and divide between 4 ramekin dishes.

3 Put the butter, sugar and syrup in a small saucepan and heat gently until melted. Remove from the heat and stir in the oats and ground ginger. Spoon this mixture over the fruit.

4 Bake for about 30 minutes, until the topping is golden. Serve with the Greek yoghurt.

'The only purple food should be in science fiction movies!'
Gregg Wallace, Masterchef Judge, to a contestant

Inspired by contestant Milla Mackey

Panettone Bread and Butter Pudding with Whisky Sauce

Panettone makes a luxurious bread and butter pudding, transforming a simple dessert into something very special indeed. The story behind it goes something like this: a poor apprentice baker found that he had no money to buy his sweetheart a Christmas present, so after he finished work on Christmas Eve he asked his boss if he could make a special present for his loved one. He baked the most beautiful light fruitcake, rich in vanilla, butter and candied peel. She, of course, was smitten.

→ 350ML (12FL OZ) MILK
→ 150ML (¼ PINT) SINGLE CREAM
→ 3 TBSP COARSE-CUT SEVILLE ORANGE MARMALADE
→ 4 EGGS
→ 200G (7OZ) PANETTONE, SLICED
→ 40G (1½OZ) UNSALTED BUTTER
→ FRESHLY GRATED NUTMEG
→ 25G (1OZ) DEMERARA SUGAR
For the whisky sauce:
→ 200G (7OZ) MASCARPONE CHEESE
→ 1 TBSP WHISKY LIQUEUR (GLAYVA OR SIMILAR)
→ 1 TBSP ICING SUGAR, SIFTED

1 Preheat the oven to 180°C/350°F/Gas Mark 4.

2 Pour the milk and cream into a saucepan and heat gently to simmering point, but do not let them boil. Add half the marmalade and stir until melted.

3 Lightly whisk the eggs together in a large bowl and pour the hot milk on to them, stirring all the time. Strain through a sieve.

4 Spread the panettone with the butter and cut it into triangles. Arrange in a buttered ovenproof dish about 23 x 18cm (9 x 7 in). Pour the egg mixture over the panettone, then finely grate a little nutmeg over and sprinkle the demerara sugar on top. Leave to stand for 10 minutes to allow the liquid to soak in.

5 Bake the pudding for 20–25 minutes, until just set and lightly browned. Meanwhile, mix all the ingredients for the whisky sauce together in a bowl.

6 Remove the pudding from the oven and brush the top with the remaining marmalade. Return to the oven for a few minutes to glaze. Serve the pudding warm, accompanied by the whisky sauce.

Individual Brioche Puddings with Caramel Sauce

This wonderful little pudding by Christopher is truly the best type of comfort food. Although it sounds similar to bread and butter pudding, the centre is more unctuous and creamy, while the outer casing of brioche becomes lovely and crisp. The caramel sauce can be used for pouring over vanilla ice cream as well as profiteroles or a classic sponge pudding.

→ A SMALL KNOB OF BUTTER FOR GREASING
→ 2 TBSP CASTER SUGAR, PLUS A LITTLE EXTRA FOR DUSTING
→ 200G (7OZ) BRIOCHE, CRUSTS REMOVED
→ 200ML (7FL OZ) WHOLE MILK
→ 300ML (½ PINT) SINGLE CREAM
→ 3 EGG YOLKS
→ 1 HEAPED TSP CORNFLOUR
→ 150G (5OZ) RAISINS
→ 1½ TSP GROUND CINNAMON
For the caramel sauce:
→ 100G (4OZ) LIGHT SOFT BROWN SUGAR
→ 50G (2OZ) UNSALTED BUTTER
→ 150ML (¼ PINT) DOUBLE CREAM

1 Preheat the oven to 180°C/350°F/Gas Mark 4. Butter 4 individual pudding bowls or ramekin dishes, about 200ml (7fl oz) in capacity, and dust them with a little caster sugar.

2 Cut the brioche into 12 thin slices and toast lightly on one side. Cut out 4 circles and use to line the base of the dishes, toasted-side down. Cut the rest of the brioche into fat 'fingers', reserving any trimmings. Use the fingers of brioche to line the sides of the dishes, toasted-side outwards. Make sure they fit snugly, with no gaps.

3 Bring the milk and single cream to boiling point in a saucepan, then cool slightly. Beat the egg yolks, cornflour and sugar together in a bowl. Slowly whisk the hot, creamy milk into the egg mixture, then strain it into a clean saucepan. Cook the custard over a low heat, stirring constantly, until it begins to thicken. Do not let it boil.

4 Remove the custard from the heat and stir in the raisins, cinnamon and brioche trimmings. The mixture should be quite sloppy. Leave to stand for 5 minutes, then spoon the mixture into the lined dishes, filling them to just below the top. Leave to stand for 10 minutes.

5 Place the dishes on a baking tray and bake for 10–15 minutes, until just set.

6 Meanwhile, make the sauce. Put all the ingredients in a heavy-based saucepan and cook over a gentle heat until the mixture is smooth and has thickened to a creamy consistency.

7 Turn the puddings out on to individual plates and pour a little caramel sauce over the top. Serve immediately.

Bakewell Tart with Quince Jam and Nibbed Almonds

Regardless of what is new and trendy, classics such as this Bakewell tart are always fantastic. Thomasina used her own quince jam but you could use any type of jam or jelly.

→ 4 TBSP QUINCE JAM
→ 40G (1½OZ) UNSALTED BUTTER, SOFTENED
→ 50G (2OZ) CASTER SUGAR
→ 1 LARGE EGG, LIGHTLY WHISKED
→ GRATED ZEST OF ½ LEMON
→ 50G (2OZ) GROUND ALMONDS
→ 40G (1½OZ) BLANCHED ALMONDS, ROUGHLY CHOPPED
→ ICING SUGAR FOR DUSTING
→ 150ML (¼ PINT) DOUBLE CREAM, TO SERVE

For the pastry:
→ 100G (4OZ) PLAIN FLOUR
→ 65G (2½OZ) UNSALTED BUTTER
→ 25G (1OZ) ICING SUGAR, SIFTED
→ 1 LARGE EGG YOLK

For the quince syrup:
→ 3 TBSP QUINCE JAM
→ 3 TBSP SAUTERNES OR OTHER SWEET WHITE WINE

1 To make the pastry, sift the flour into a bowl and rub in the butter until the mixture resembles fine breadcrumbs. Stir in the icing sugar, followed by the egg yolk and mix to a firm dough. Cover with cling film and chill for 30 minutes.

2 Roll out the pastry on a lightly floured surface and use to line a lightly greased 18cm (7 in) flan tin. Chill for 10 minutes.

3 Preheat the oven to 180°C/350°F/Gas Mark 4. Gently melt the quince jam in a small pan and spread it over the base of the pastry case. Return the pastry case to the fridge.

4 Beat the butter and caster sugar together in a bowl until light and fluffy. Beat in the egg, lemon zest and ground almonds, then stir in the blanched almonds.

5 Pour this mixture into the pastry case and bake for about 25 minutes, until it turns a light golden brown. The filling should be just set and not too firm. Remove the tart from the oven and leave to rest for 5 minutes, then transfer to a wire rack and leave to cool completely. Dust with icing sugar.

6 Put the quince jam and Sauternes in a small saucepan and stir over a low heat until the jam has melted to form a syrup. Serve the Bakewell tart at room temperature, with the quince syrup and double cream.

Masterchef Masterclass
John Torode's Pastry

Making pastry is a fantastic skill to master. It isn't difficult and it opens the way to so many different dishes, from robust savoury pies and pasties to refined quiches and the entire range of sweet tarts. Very few pastry products that you buy in the shops can equal a home-made tart or pie straight from the oven.

Whatever type of pastry you are making, the aim is a crisp, light result. This is achieved by using soft flour (i.e. ordinary plain white flour), which is low in gluten, and a high proportion of fat to give a characteristic 'short' texture. Butter gives the best flavour and colour, although some savoury pastries include lard for a flaky texture. A little liquid, usually water or egg, binds the dough. If you use egg, it also enriches it and makes it more pliable.

Pastry should be mixed quickly and lightly so the gluten in the flour doesn't develop too much, otherwise the dough will be stretchy and more likely to shrink during cooking. You don't need a marble worktop: although it is correct that the ingredients, especially for sweet and shortcrust pastry, should be cool, the most important thing is to get the proportions right – no amount of cooling will help if you put too much butter in the mixture

Many people are nervous about trying pastry recipes, but there are a few steps that you can follow to take the pressure off and allow you to relax and be confident of success:

→ Be gentle with pastry and the results will be perfect.
→ Get to know your oven and its peculiarities – particularly if you use a fan oven, where you may have to adjust the temperature.
→ Keep your work surface and tart tins spotlessly clean.
→ Keep all your ingredients cool, including the flour.
→ Cold hands are important, too. If you have warm hands, run them under the cold tap for a minute or so and dry them well before you start making pastry.
→ Tough pastry comes from being worked too much, so mix it quickly and lightly and roll it out only once.
→ Use a cool, well-floured work surface for rolling out.
→ Grease the tin with the smallest possible amount of butter.
→ Pre-bake the pastry before adding the filling (this is known as baking blind), for a crisp outer shell without a soggy bottom.

John Torode's
Sweet Shortcrust Pastry

→ 150G (5OZ) UNSALTED BUTTER
→ 300G (10OZ) PLAIN WHITE FLOUR
→ 100G (4OZ) CASTER SUGAR
→ GRATED ZEST OF 1 LEMON
→ 2 MEDIUM EGGS

This is based on the traditional French pâte sucrée, with a high proportion of sugar and egg for a rich, biscuity texture. It is the base for all those great classic sweet tarts, from a sharp, tangy lemon tart to the perfect chocolate tart.

1 Dice the butter and leave it to soften at room temperature for 30 minutes.

2 Sift the flour into a large bowl, make a well in the centre and add the butter and sugar. Work in the butter with your fingertips until the mixture resembles fine breadcrumbs. Stir in the lemon zest.

3 Break in the eggs and, using your fingertips, bring everything together. Turn out on to a floured work surface and knead lightly by pushing the dough away with the heel of your hand 3 times, giving it a quarter turn each time. You should end up with a silky-smooth ball of dough.

4 Wrap the pastry in cling film and leave it to rest in the fridge for about an hour before using (it will keep in the fridge for 3–4 days at this stage and also freezes well).

5 Unwrap the pastry and place it on a lightly floured work surface. Gently push down on the pastry with a rolling pin, then give it a quarter turn and repeat. Do this 4 times, so the pastry begins to flatten out.

6 Start to roll out the pastry, moving it around on the work surface from time to time to prevent sticking; if necessary, dust the work surface and the rolling pin with more flour. Roll out to about 5mm ($^1/_4$ in) thick (if you become nervous about it tearing, you can always stop before it gets this thin).

7 Lift the pastry up on the rolling pin and lay it over a lightly greased 25cm (10 in) loose-bottomed fluted tart tin. Ease the pastry down the sides to fit the tin, being careful to push it right down into the corners and making sure there are no

gaps between the pastry and the tin. Instead of using warm fingers, which may melt the pastry, you could make a small ball of excess dough and use it to press the pastry gently into the tin. Lightly run the rolling pin over the top of the tin to remove excess pastry, then push the pastry up slightly all the way round, if possible, so it is a little higher than the side of the tin. Chill for about 10 minutes.

8 To bake blind, preheat the oven to 200°C/400°F/Gas Mark 6 and place a baking sheet in it. Line the pastry case with a sheet of baking parchment, bringing it right up the sides. Fill with dried beans or rice, then place in the oven on the hot baking sheet and bake for 15 minutes, until the base of the pastry case is pale and chalky looking.

9 Remove the paper and filling (the beans or rice can be reused whenever you make pastry) and reduce the oven temperature to 150°C/300°F/Gas Mark 2. Return the pastry case to the oven for 15 minutes, until the base is a uniform pale-golden brown. Leave to cool.

Lemon and Plum Tart with Crème Fraîche

This tart relies upon frangipane, an almond and butter paste, to give it body and form. If you can't get plums, then apricots or nectarines would work just as well.

- → 75G (3OZ) UNSALTED BUTTER, SOFTENED
- → 100G (4OZ) CASTER SUGAR
- → 2 LARGE EGGS, LIGHTLY BEATEN
- → GRATED ZEST OF 1 LEMON
- → 100G (4OZ) GROUND ALMONDS
- → 3 PLUMS, HALVED, STONED AND CUT INTO 6 WEDGES EACH
- → 4 TBSP MELTED BUTTER
- → 1 TSP ICING SUGAR
- → 150ML (¼ PINT) CRÈME FRAÎCHE

For the pastry:
- → 200G (7OZ) PLAIN FLOUR
- → 90G (3OZ) UNSALTED BUTTER
- → 40G (1½OZ) CASTER SUGAR
- → 1 MEDIUM EGG, LIGHTLY BEATEN

1 First make the pastry. Sift the flour into a bowl and rub in the butter with your fingertips until the mixture resembles fine breadcrumbs. Stir in the sugar. Add the egg and mix to a firm dough. Cover with cling film and chill for 30 minutes.

2 Roll out the pastry on a floured surface and use to line a lightly greased deep 18cm (7 in) flan tin. Chill for 10 minutes.

3 Preheat the oven to 180°C/350°F/Gas Mark 4. For the filling, cream the butter and caster sugar together in a bowl until light and fluffy. Beat in the eggs, a little at a time, followed by the lemon zest and ground almonds.

4 Pour this almond cream into the pastry case and arrange the plums on top, overlapping them slightly. Brush with the melted butter and sift the icing sugar over the fruit.

5 Bake for 20–25 minutes, until the almond cream swells up around the fruit and turns a light golden brown. Remove the tart from the oven and leave to rest for 5 minutes. Transfer to a wire rack and leave to cool. Serve at room temperature, accompanied by the crème fraîche.

Blackberry Shortcakes with Blackberry and Orange Compote

This is one of the Masterchef crew's favourites, not because it is the work of a culinary genius but because it is the greatest comfort food ever made. It's a simple, scone-like affair served with fresh blackberries and an orange-flavoured blackberry compote. You can make the shortcakes large or small, but smaller ones are prettier.

- 250G (9OZ) BLACKBERRIES
- 1½ TBSP CASTER SUGAR
- GRATED ZEST AND JUICE OF 1 ORANGE
- 150ML (¼ PINT) DOUBLE CREAM

For the shortcakes:
- 175G (6OZ) PLAIN FLOUR
- A PINCH OF SALT
- 1½ TSP BAKING POWDER
- 75G (3OZ) UNSALTED BUTTER, FINELY DICED
- 1½ TBSP CASTER SUGAR, PLUS A LITTLE EXTRA FOR SPRINKLING
- 1 SMALL EGG
- 1 TBSP SINGLE CREAM
- 1 EGG WHITE, LIGHTLY BEATEN

MASTERCHEF TOP TIP

Shortcake is a delightful dessert, not to be confused with shortbread – it's actually more like a scone. Be careful not to overwork the dough, as this will make the cake tough and cause it to shrink as it cooks. A light, aerated mixture is most important.

When cooking the compote, try to keep the definition of the fruit, as this looks more attractive.

Peter Richards, Masterchef Mentor

1 Preheat the oven to 180°C/350°F/Gas Mark 4.

2 To make the shortcakes, sift the flour, salt and baking powder into a large bowl and add the butter and sugar. Rub in the butter until the mixture resembles fine breadcrumbs. Whisk the egg and single cream together and stir into the flour mixture to form a dough. Cover and chill for 30 minutes.

3 On a lightly floured work surface, roll out the dough to 2cm (¾ in) thick. Cut out 4 rounds using a 6.5cm (2 ½ in) cutter. Place on a greased baking sheet, brush with the egg white and sprinkle with a little sugar. Bake for 10–15 minutes, until light golden brown, then leave to cool.

4 For the compote, put half the blackberries in a saucepan with the sugar, orange zest and juice. Cover and cook gently for a few minutes, until the fruit is tender but still holds its shape. Leave to cool.

5 Whip the double cream until it forms soft peaks. Split the shortcakes in half and fill with the cream and fresh blackberries. Drizzle the compote around the shortcakes and serve.

'[That] pud was simple: a perfect understanding of ingredients and how they work.'
Gregg Wallace, Masterchef Judge

Cranachan with Raspberry Tuiles

Cranachan is a classic that's eaten all over Scotland, where it was originally served as a celebration of 'harvest home'.

The quality of the raspberries is crucial to the success of this dish. If they are not ripe and sweet, the whisky and oatmeal cream will overpower, rather than complement them. It is said that Scottish raspberries are the best in the world, so look out for them in late summer and early autumn.

→ 50G (2OZ) PINHEAD OATMEAL
→ 300ML (½ PINT) DOUBLE CREAM
→ 2 TSP CASTER SUGAR
→ 2–3 TBSP DRAMBUIE OR GLAYVA
→ 1 TBSP RUNNY HONEY
→ 1 PUNNET OF FRESH RASPBERRIES
→ ICING SUGAR FOR DUSTING
  For the tuiles:
→ 2 EGG WHITES
→ 75G (3OZ) ICING SUGAR
→ 50G (2OZ) PLAIN FLOUR, SIFTED
→ 50G (2OZ) UNSALTED BUTTER, MELTED

MASTERCHEF TOP TIP
To make all the tuile biscuits exactly the same size, trim the edges off a plastic ice-cream lid to create a flat piece of plastic, then draw the size and shape of tuile required on it. Cut the shape out and lay the remaining plastic on the baking sheet. Use a spatula to fill the cut-out area with the biscuit mix, then run the spatula over the top to remove any excess.
John Torode, Masterchef Judge

1 Preheat the oven to 180°C/350°F/Gas Mark 4.

2 For the tuiles, put the egg whites in a bowl, sift in the icing sugar and whisk for 10–15 seconds. Sift in the flour, gently pour in the melted butter and mix to a smooth paste.

3 On a baking tray lined with baking parchment, spread the mixture out into four 10–12cm (4–4½ in) discs with the back of a spoon, leaving space between them so they can spread (any leftover mixture will keep in the fridge for a week).

4 Bake for 8–10 minutes, until the tuiles are golden brown and beginning to bubble. Remove from the oven and drape each one over a lightly greased small, upturned cup or ramekin while still warm. Once cool and crisp, remove from the cup (they will stay crisp for up to 48 hours in an airtight container).

5 Spread the oatmeal out on a baking sheet and toast in the oven for 8–10 minutes, until golden brown. Leave to cool.

6 Whip the double cream, caster sugar, Drambuie and honey together until the mixture just holds its shape. Fold in the toasted oatmeal and then chill.

7 To serve, put a few raspberries into each tuile and top with the cranachan. Decorate with the remaining raspberries and dust with icing sugar. Serve immediately.

Tangerine Soufflé

Some people are intimidated by the thought of making a soufflé but there is no need to be. A soufflé is simply a baked dessert that uses lots of egg white to make it rise. Once you have whipped your egg whites properly, there are two things needed to stop a soufflé collapsing – a steady cooking temperature and a non-convection oven, otherwise the vibrations of the oven can destabilise the mixture and cause the top to fall off. Lastly, make sure that there is a good amount of flavouring, or the soufflé will taste too eggy.

→ A KNOB OF BUTTER FOR GREASING
→ 2 TBSP CASTER SUGAR, PLUS EXTRA FOR DUSTING
→ 1 TBSP TANGERINE MARMALADE
→ 2 TBSP FRESH TANGERINE JUICE (OR ORANGE JUICE)
→ 1 TBSP COINTREAU
→ 2 LARGE EGG WHITES
→ 4 AMARETTI BISCUITS

MASTERCHEF TOP TIP
There is no mystery to making a hot soufflé, and it is a wonderful way to finish a meal. Make it with confidence and don't be afraid of the ingredients. The crucial thing is to whip the egg whites to the correct consistency – they should form stiff peaks. Always make sure the whisk and bowl are spotlessly clean. If you add a little lemon juice to the egg whites before whisking, it will make them stronger.
Peter Richards, Masterchef Mentor

1 Preheat the oven to 180°C/350°F/Gas Mark 4. Grease 4 ramekin dishes with the butter and dust thoroughly with caster sugar, then set aside.

2 Put the marmalade into a small saucepan with the tangerine juice and Cointreau and bring to the boil. Remove from the heat and stir to break down the marmalade. Transfer to a small saucer and leave to cool, but do not let it set.

3 Whisk the egg whites in a clean bowl until stiff. With a large metal spoon, lightly fold in the caster sugar and the cooled tangerine mixture.

4 Divide the mixture between the ramekins, leaving the rim clear. Put the dishes on a baking sheet and bake for 8 minutes, until well risen and golden brown on top. Serve immediately, with the amaretti biscuits.

Summer Berry Sabayon

If you're Italian, you will recognise the sabayon sauce as a zabaglione. The secret to getting this fluffy, delicious warm sauce right is in the whisking. You have to make sure that the mixture is whisked long enough for it to become the consistency of double cream. The addition of Frangelico is inspired, giving it a wonderful hazelnut flavour. You could use other liqueurs, such as Grand Marnier or kirsch, or marsala.

→ 4 EGG YOLKS
→ 60G (2¼OZ) CASTER SUGAR
→ 5 TBSP FRANGELICO (HAZELNUT LIQUEUR)
→ 300G (11OZ) MIXED SUMMER BERRIES, SUCH AS RASPBERRIES, STRAWBERRIES AND BLACKBERRIES
→ 2 TBSP FLAKED ALMONDS
→ MINT SPRIGS, TO DECORATE

1 Preheat the grill. Put the egg yolks and sugar in a large bowl and whisk until pale and thick, using a hand-held electric beater.

2 Add the Frangelico and place the bowl over a saucepan of gently simmering water, making sure the water doesn't touch the base of the bowl. Continue whisking for at least 10 minutes, until the mixture is pale and very foamy. It should have increased in volume dramatically.

3 Put the mixed berries into a heatproof serving dish. Spoon the sabayon over the fruit and sprinkle the almonds on top.

4 Place under a hot grill for 2–3 minutes, until the almonds and sabayon colour slightly. Decorate with sprigs of mint and serve immediately.

Inspired by contestant Caroline Brewester

Sparkling Cranberry Jellies with Orange Langue de Chat Biscuits

The key to success here is to let the mixture cool before adding the wine, so all the bubbles set with the jelly rather then being destroyed by the heat. Remember that these jellies are alcoholic and therefore should be served in little glasses.

- → 350ML (12FL OZ) GOOD-QUALITY CRANBERRY JUICE DRINK
- → 200G (7OZ) FRESH CRANBERRIES
- → 200G (7OZ) GRANULATED SUGAR
- → 6 GELATINE LEAVES
- → ABOUT ½ BOTTLE OF DRY CAVA OR OTHER DRY SPARKLING WINE
- → 4 SMALL SPRIGS OF MINT

For the biscuits:
- → GRATED ZEST OF 1 ORANGE
- → 60G (2¼OZ) UNSALTED BUTTER, SOFTENED
- → 60G (2¼OZ) CASTER SUGAR
- → 2 EGG WHITES, LIGHTLY BEATEN
- → 60G (2¼OZ) PLAIN FLOUR

1 Pour 300ml (½ pint) of the cranberry juice into a saucepan and add the cranberries and sugar. Bring to the boil, then reduce the heat and simmer for 5 minutes, until the cranberries are soft. Remove from the heat.

2 Soak the gelatine leaves in the remaining cranberry juice for 5 minutes. Meanwhile, strain the cranberries and juice through a fine sieve into a large basin, pressing the cranberries with the back of a spoon to extract all the liquid. Measure the strained liquid; you should have about 500ml (18fl oz).

3 Add the soaked gelatine to the hot liquid, stirring until dissolved. Leave to cool.

4 Make the liquid up to 900ml (1½ pints) with the Cava and stir until thoroughly combined. Let the bubbles subside, then pour into four 250ml (8fl oz) glasses. Chill until set.

5 Preheat the oven to 200°C/400°F/Gas Mark 6. For the biscuits, put the orange zest and butter into a bowl and beat well. Add the sugar and beat until pale and fluffy. Stir in the egg whites (the mixture will look slightly curdled), then beat in the flour, mixing to a fairly stiff cream.

6 Fit a piping bag with a small nozzle and fill with the mixture. Line a baking sheet with baking parchment and pipe thin strips of the mixture on to it, about 5cm (2 in) long. They will spread dramatically in the oven, so leave 5cm (2 in) between each one.

7 Bake for about 8 minutes, until they are pale gold in the centre and darker at the edges. Transfer to a wire rack to cool.

8 Serve the sparkling cranberry jellies decorated with the sprigs of mint and accompanied by the biscuits.

Avocado and Honey Ice Cream with Caramelised Aubergine

Now this is a real left-field recipe but, in the true spirit of Masterchef, Christopher wanted to push the boat out and try something different. It works surprisingly well. If you like to be innovative in your cooking, do give it a go. It might be fun not to tell people what you are serving them, to see if they can guess what it is.

- → 300ML (½ PINT) MILK
- → 300ML (½ PINT) DOUBLE CREAM
- → 6 MEDIUM EGG YOLKS
- → 175G (6OZ) CASTER SUGAR
- → 2 AVOCADOS
- → 4 TBSP RUNNY HONEY
  For the caramelised aubergines:
- → 2 TBSP CLARIFIED BUTTER
- → 3 TBSP CASTER SUGAR
- → 8 SLICES OF AUBERGINE, CUT 8MM (⅓ IN) THICK

1 Bring the milk and cream to simmering point in a saucepan. Whisk the egg yolks and caster sugar together until pale and very thick, using a hand-held electric beater. Pour the hot (but not boiling) cream on to the egg yolk mixture, stirring vigorously until well blended.

2 Pour the mixture into a clean pan and cook over a very low heat, stirring constantly, until the custard thickens enough to coat the back of the spoon; do not let it boil. Cool the mixture down quickly by placing the pan in a sink of cold water, stirring occasionally.

3 When the custard is cold, peel and stone the avocados, then purée them in a blender or food processor with the honey. Stir into the custard, mixing well.

4 Pour the custard into an ice-cream maker and churn for 20 minutes or until it has thickened and increased in volume but not frozen completely. Pour into a container and finish in the freezer.

5 For the caramelised aubergines, melt the clarified butter in a large, non-stick frying pan over a low heat. Sprinkle half the caster sugar over the aubergine slices. Add the slices to the pan (in batches, if necessary), sugar-side down, and cook until they go a deep golden brown underneath. Sprinkle the rest of the sugar on top, then turn them over and cook until browned and tender. Serve warm, with the avocado ice cream.

List of Suppliers with Introduction by Gregg Wallace

LONDON

Bread and Patisserie

& Clarke's
122 Kensington Church Street,
London W8 4BH
Tel: 020 7229 2190
www.sallyclarke.com

Baker and Spice
75 Salusbury Road, London NW6 6NH
Tel: 020 7664 3636
www.bakerandspice.com

De Gustibus
53 Blandford Street, London W1H 3AF
Tel: 020 7486 6608

Euphorium Bakery
203 Upper Street, London N1 1RQ
Tel: 020 7704 6905

Konditor and Cook
10 Stoney Street, London SE1 9AD
Tel: 020 7407 5100

Lighthouse Bakery
64 Northcote Road, London SW11 6QL
Tel: 020 7228 4537
www.lighthousebakery.co.uk

Ottolenghi
287 Upper Street, London N1 2TZ
Tel: 020 7288 1454
www.ottolenghi.co.uk

Poilâne
46 Elizabeth Street, London SW1W 9PA
Tel: 020 7808 4910
www.poilane.fr

Cheese and Dairy

La Fromagerie
2–4 Moxon Street, London W1U 4EW
Tel: 020 7935 0341
www.lafromagerie.co.uk

Neal's Yard Dairy
6 Park Street, London SE1 9AB
Tel: 020 7645 3550
www.nealsyarddairy.co.uk

Paxton & Whitfield
93 Jermyn Street, London SW1Y 6JE
Tel: 020 7930 0259
www.paxtonandwhitfield.co.uk

Delicatessens and Specialist Foods

Alford's of Farringdon
506 Central Markets, Farringdon Road,
London EC1A 9NL

Arigato
48–50 Brewer Street, London W1F 9TG
Tel: 020 7287 1722

Brindisa
32 Exmouth Market, London EC1R 4QE
Tel: 020 7713 1666
www.brindisa.com

Carluccio's Caffé
Branches across the South-East
www.carluccios.com

Comptoir Gascon
63 Charterhouse Street,
London EC1M 6HJ
Tel: 020 7608 0851

Del'Aziz
24–28 Vanston Place, London SW6 1AX
Tel: 020 7386 0086

The Grocer on Elgin
6 Elgin Crescent, Notting Hill W11 2HX
Tel: 020 7221 3844
www.thegroceron.com

Jeroboams
96 Holland Park Avenue,
London W11 3RB
Tel: 020 7727 9359

Elizabeth King
34 New Kings Road, London SW6 4ST
Tel: 020 7736 2826

Megan's
571 Kings Road, London SW6 2EB
Tel: 020 7371 7837

Monte's
Canonbury Lane, London N1 2AS
Tel: 020 7354 4335

Mortimer & Bennett
33 Turnham Green Terrace,
London W4 1RG
Tel: 020 8995 4145
www.mortimerandbennett.com

Olga Stores
30 Penton Street, London N1 9PS
Tel: 020 7837 5467

Panzer's
13–19 Circus Road, London NW8 6PB
Tel: 020 7722 8596
www.panzers.co.uk

Petit Luc's Delicatessen
4 Leadenhall Market, London EC3V 1LR
Tel: 020 7283 6707

Speck
2 Holland Park Terrace,
Portland Road, London W11 4ND
Tel: 020 7229 7005
www.speck-deli.co.uk

The Spice Shop
1 Blenheim Crescent,
London W11 2EE
Tel: 020 7221 4448
www.thespiceshop.co.uk

Taj Stores
112–114 Brick Lane, London E1 6RL
Tel: 020 7377 0061

Villandry
170 Great Portland Street,
London W1W 5QB
Tel: 020 7631 3131
www.villandry.com

Fish

Chalmers & Gray
67 Notting Hill Gate, London W11 3JS
Tel: 020 7221 6177

Cope's
700 Fulham Road, London SW6 5SA
Tel: 020 7371 7300

Steve Hatt
88–90 Essex Road, London N1 8LU
Tel: 020 7226 3963

H. S. Linwood & Sons
6–7 Leadenhall Market,
London EC3V 1LR
Tel: 020 7929 0554

Food Halls

Flâneur Food Hall
41 Farringdon Road, London EC1M 3JB
Tel: 020 7404 4422

Fortnum and Mason
181 Piccadilly, London W1A 1ER
Tel: 020 7734 8040
www.fortnumandmason.com

Harrods
87–135 Brompton Road,
London SW1X 7XL
Tel: 020 7730 1234
www.harrods.com

Selfridges
400 Oxford Street, London W1A 2LR
Tel: 020 7629 1234
www.selfridges.co.uk

Fruit and Vegetables

Barbican Fruiterers and Greengrocers
26 Goswell Road, London EC1M 7AA
Tel: 020 7253 2190

Michanicou Brothers
2 Clarendon Road, London W11 3AA
Tel: 020 7727 5191

Susan's
234 Essex Road, London N1 3AP
Tel: 020 7226 6844

Meat, Poultry and Game

Allen & Co.
117 Mount Street, London W1K 3LA
Tel: 020 7499 5831

S. C. Crosby
65 Charterhouse Street,
London EC1M 6HJ
Tel: 020 7253 1239

A. Dove and Son
71 Northcote Road, London SW11 6PJ
Tel: 020 7223 5191

James Elliot
96 Essex Road, London N1 8LU
Tel: 020 7226 3658

The Ginger Pig
8–10 Moxon Street, London W1U 4EU
Tel: 020 7935 7788

Frank Godfrey
7 Highbury Park, London N5 1QJ
Tel: 020 7226 9904

A. A. King
30–34 New King Road,
London SW6 4ST
Tel: 020 7736 4004

C. Lidgate
110 Holland Park Avenue,
London W11 4UA
Tel: 020 7727 8243

Meat City
507 Central Markets,
Farringdon Road, London EC1A 9NL
Tel: 020 7253 9606

M. Moen & Sons
24 The Pavement, London SW4 0JA
Tel: 020 7622 1624

E. Wood
53 Barnsbury Street, London N1 1TP
Tel: 020 7607 1522

Wine and Spirits

La Grande Marque
55 Leadenhall Market,
London EC3V 1LT
Tel: 020 7929 3536

Lea & Sandeman
211 Kensington Church Street,
London W8 7LX
Tel: 020 7221 1982
www.londonfinewines.co.uk

Milroys of Soho
3 Greek Street, London W1V 6NX
Tel: 020 7437 9311
www.milroys.co.uk

Markets

Borough Market
8 Southwark Street, London SE1 1TL
Tel: 020 7404 1002
www.boroughmarket.org.uk

Chapel Market
Conduit Street, Grant Street and
Baron Street, London N1 9EX

North End Road Market
North End Road, London SW6 1NL
Tel: 020 8748 3020

REST OF BRITAIN AND IRELAND

*This barely scratches the surface
of the fantastic selection of suppliers
around the country, but should give
you somewhere to start! Many suppliers
offer a mail-order service.*

Bread and Patisseries

S. C. Price & Sons
7 Castle Street, Ludlow SY8 1AS
Tel: 01584 872815

Shipton Mill
Long Newnton, Tetbury GL8 8RP
Tel: 01666 505050

The Village Bakery
Melmerby, Penrith CA10 1HE
Tel: 01768 881811
www.village-bakery.com

Cheese and Dairy

The Cheese Shop
116 Northgate Street, Chester CH1 2HT
Tel: 01244 346240
www.chestercheeseshop.com

The Fine Cheese Company
29 & 31 Walcot Street, Bath BA1 5BN
Tel: 01225 448748
www.finecheese.co.uk

The House of Cheese
13 Church Street, Tetbury GL8 8JG
Tel: 01666 502865
www.houseofcheese.co.uk

I. J. Mellis
492 Great Western Road,
Glasgow G12 8EW
Tel: 0141 339 8998
www.ijmellischeesemonger.com

Delicatessens and Specialist Foods

Lewis & Cooper
92 High Street, Northallerton DL7 8PP
Tel: 01609 772880
www.lewis-and-cooper.co.uk

Provender
3 Market Square,
South Petherton TA13 5BT
Tel: 01460 240681
www.provender.net

Real Eating Company
86–87 Western Road, Hove BN3 1JB
Tel: 01273 221444
www.real-eating.co.uk

Valvona & Crolla
19 Elm Row, Edinburgh EH7 4AA
Tel: 0131 556 6066
www.valvonacrolla.co.uk

The Vineyard Delicatessen
23–24 Eld Lane, Colchester CO1 1LS
Tel: 01206 573363
www.vineyard-deli.co.uk

Fish

Fishworks
6 Green Street, Bath BA1 2JY
Tel: 01225 448707
*Branches in Bristol, Christchurch
and London*
http://www.fishworks.co.uk

John's Fish Shop Suffolk
5 East Street,
Southwold IP18 6EH
Tel: 01502 724253
www.johns-fish-shop.co.uk

Simply Organic Food Company
Horsley Road, Kingsthorpe Hollow,
Northampton NN2 6LJ
Tel: 0870 7606001
www.simplyorganic.net

Whitstable Shellfish Company
Westmead Road, Whitstable CT5 1LW
Tel: 01227 282375
www.whitstable-shellfish.co.uk

Fruit and Vegetables

Abel & Cole
www.abel-cole.co.uk

Howbarrow Organic Farm
Cartmel,
Grange-over-Sands LA11 7SS
Tel: 01539 536330
www.howbarroworganic.demon.co.uk

The Organic Farm Shop
Abbey Home Farm,
Burford Road, Cirencester GL7 5HF
Tel: 01285 640441
www.theorganicfarmshop.co.uk

Peppers by Post
Sea Spring Farm,
West Bexington, Dorchester DT2 9DD
Tel: 01308 897892
www.peppersbypost.biz

Secretts Direct
www.secrettsdirect.co.uk

Meat, Poultry and Game

Alternative Meats
Hough Farm,
Weston-under-Redcastle,
Shrewsbury SY4 5LR
Tel: 011948 840130
www.alternativemeats.co.uk

The Butts Farm Shop
South Cerney, Cirencester GL7 5QE
Tel: 01255 862224
www.buttsfarmshop.com

Kelly Turkey Farms
Springate Farm,
Bicknacre Road, Danbury CM3 4EP
Tel: 01245 223581
www.kelly-turkeys.com

Langley Chase Organic Farm
Kington Langley SN15 5PW
Tel: 01249 750 095
www.langleychase.co.uk

Swaddles Green Organic Farm
Chard TA20 3JR
Tel: 0845 456 1768
www.swaddles.co.uk

G. & R. Tudge
The Bury, Richards Castle,
Ludlow SY8 4EL
Tel: 01584 831227

D. W. Wall
14 High St, Ludlow SY8 1BS
Tel: 01584 872060

Supermarkets

Marks and Spencer
Tel: 0845 302 1234
www.marksandspencer.com

Sainsburys
Tel: 0800 636262
www.sainsburys.co.uk

Waitrose
Tel: 0800 188 884
www.waitrose.com

Wines, Beers and Spirits

Berry Bros & Rudd
Tel: 0870 900 4300
www.bbr.com

Oddbins
Tel: 0800 328 2323
www.oddbins.com

Threshers
Tel: 01707 387200
www.threshers.co.uk

Index